What Every Well-Informed Person Should Know About Drug Addiction

What Every Well-Informed Person Should Know About Drug Addiction

David P. Ausubel M.D., Ph.D.

Nelson-Hall nh Chicago

Library of Congress Cataloging in Publication Data

Ausubel, David Paul.
What every well-informed person should know about drug addiction.

Bibliography: p.
Includes index.
1. Narcotic habit. 2. Consumer education.
I. Title. [DNLM: 1. Drug dependence. WM270.3 A938d]
RC566.A86   613.8'3   79-16961
ISBN 0-88229-566-7 (cloth)
ISBN 0-88229-721-x (paper)

Manufactured in the United States of America

10   9   8   7   6   5   4   3   2   1

To:
My thousands of drug-addict patients
from 1946 to 1978

Contents

Preface to the Second Edition

Since the appearance of the first edition of this book in 1958, the problem of drug addiction has grown much more serious. The 1960s and early 1970s saw an epidemic of drug addiction which dwarfed by comparison the post-World War II addiction epidemic. The problem then and now (since the 1960s) is largely a problem of urban slum areas, and more nearly involves teen-agers and young adults, particularly blacks and persons of Puerto Rican and Mexican ancestry although it has also spread to the suburbs and small towns.

In the urban ghettoes, drug addiction is endemic and coexistent with such problems as poverty, inadequate housing, unemployment, and racism. Nevertheless, its incidence is still selective, based on personality predisposition; for, although nearly all teen-agers in these areas experiment with drugs at one time or another, relatively few become physiologically and psychologically addicted to them. In part this experimentation with drugs is a reflection of the general culture's *legal* abuse of mood-changing drugs (e.g., alcohol, sedatives, tranquilizers). In part it is a reflection of youth's partial alienation from the values of the dominant adult culture.

Other differences in the drug scene since 1958 are (1) the widespread use of LSD in the late 1960s and its dramatic curtailment several years later; (2) the almost universal experimentation with and/or social use of marihuana by the youth culture; and (3) the widespread abuse of alcohol, barbiturates, minor tranquilizers (e.g. Valium®, and Librium®), hypnotics (like Placidyl®, Methaqualone®, and Doriden®), cocaine, and the amphetamines for euphoric purposes.*

---

* Since this book has gone to press, the Drug Enforcement Administration has reported a significant increase in drug addiction among women and white middle-class persons, and in small towns and suburban areas. Similar findings were reported in Boston (*The Evening Globe*, April 22, 1975) and in Washington, D. C. (*The Washington Star*, May 15, 1975). A steady increase in drug use by metropolitan Toronto high-school students from 1968 to 1974 at all grade levels was reported by Smart et al., 1974.

Drug addiction, in all likelihood, will be a problem in the United States for many years to come. The decrease in heroin addiction in the early 1970s (following the temporary ban on the opium crop in Turkey) has been more than compensated for by the increase in primary methadone addiction, polydrug abuse, and the greatly increased use of cocaine.*

As long as there is an oversupply of illicit drugs, community tolerance of drug abuse among certain ethnic groups and social classes, the existence of motivationally inadequate personalities (on genic, subcultural, or child-rearing grounds), urban slums (populated by culturally unassimilated ethnic or racial groups), and corrupt law-enforcement officials, there will always be drug addicts.

Nevertheless, although the number of drug addicts has increased tenfold in the last two decades, relapse rates among adequately treated addicts have dropped from 95 percent to 35 percent. And there is reason to believe, from past and current law enforcement experience in such countries as China, that with firm and honest law-enforcement measures decreasing the availability of illicit drugs, the incidence of drug addiction can be reduced from a figure approaching 20 percent of the total population to nearly zero. This goal is possible, despite widespread personality predispositions toward addiction and favorable cultural attitudes toward addiction, if access to drugs is minimized.

Uncritical and naive cross-cultural comparisons of the ways of socially managing drug addiction are misleading. Persons who advocate, for example, the importation of the more permissive British approach into the United States conveniently forget (1) that the addiction rate in the United Kingdom was always extremely low (both *before* and after the adoption of the permissive approach), (2) that cultural disapproval of drug addiction was always much more stringent in Great Britain than in the United States, (3) that Britain's population does not consist of 16 percent unassimilated ethnic and racial groups concentrated in the urban slums, and (4) that Britain is a sociologically much more stable and homogeneous culture than the United States (as demonstrated by the lower rates

---

* A report by the White House Special Action Office for Drug Abuse Prevention indicates an increase in heroin, marihuana, cocaine, barbiturate, and amphetamine use from 1969-1974, although there are signs that this has peaked (*New York Times*, Sunday, July 6, 1975).

of crime, divorce, and alcoholism). They also fail to point out that Britain's Crown Colony of Hong Kong, which has a higher addiction rate than the United States, does not employ the permissive approach of the mother country but much more rigorous law-enforcement practices similar to those of the United States.

It must surely be realized by all well-informed persons in the field of drug addiction that corrupt law enforcement and obscene profits in drug trafficking only exacerbate the drug addiction problem rather than cause it. No matter how predisposed a person may be to drug addiction by virtue of personality make-up or cultural attitudes, he cannot become addicted as long as illicit drugs are not available. Historical experience all over the world (including the United States and China) amply demonstrates the truth of this statement. For society to take a permissive attitude toward a practice that is so destructive of individual self-realization and cultural well-being is truly socially immoral.

Thus, it is extremely difficult to understand the position of many well-intentioned but misguided psychiatrists, psychologists, lawyers, and social scientists who advocate the elimination of all restrictive legal controls on drug abuse and the legalization of the drug habit (e.g., provision of free heroin to all addicts who apply for it), and who claim that law enforcement and the prospect of huge illicit drug profits (rather than personality predispositions, community tolerance, and drug availability) create the drug addiction problem. Even in countries like Great Britain, Sweden, and Israel, where the social climate for a more permissive approach is more favorable than in the United States, temporary relaxation of the laws against drug abuse has eradicated neither the drug addiction problem nor the illicit traffic in drugs. In recent years, the tendency in these countries has been to increase the stringency of the Dangerous Drugs laws.

Thus, like the first edition, this edition will take a definite theoretical orientation and philosophical approach toward the drug addiction problem, rather than an eclectic, controversy-free stance. In addition, it will include all new developments in the field since 1958 and devote more attention to the nonopiate forms of addiction which have become so prevalent in recent years, and (as in the 1958 edition) it will use relatively nontechnical language throughout.

From 1968 to the present, I have extended my personal knowledge of and experience with drug addiction in the urban slums by working as a psychiatrist in New York with black and Puerto Rican addicts in Harlem, and since 1975 mainly with middle-class addicts in Elmhurst and Corona. To my colleagues and patients in both the drug-free and Methadone Maintenance Treatment Programs of the Drug Abuse Control Commission of New York State, and in the two Methadone Maintenance Treatment Programs of the Mt. Sinai Hospital Services, City Hospital Center at Elmhurst, I owe a great debt of gratitude for whatever insights I have gained into this psychosocial problem of multiple causality. However, I take sole responsibility for the opinions expressed in this volume.

New York City, January 1978   David P. Ausubel, M.D., Ph.D.

Preface to the First Edition

There are few great public health and social issues of our times about which professional and lay persons are as poorly informed or misinformed as drug addiction. The medical literature is relatively inaccessible. It is scattered widely in obscure and little-read journals and tends to be extremely technical and esoteric to the uninitiated. On the other hand, ample sources of misinformation are available. The lurid and sensational features of drug addiction provide a favorite theme for the Sunday supplements of our less responsible newspapers. During the teen-age "epidemic" of drug addiction in 1950–1951, tons of misinformation were foisted upon the American public by radio commentators, newspaper columnists, and special feature writers. Lacking easy access to reliable and scientific data, these persons turned to the drug addicts themselves in their desperate effort to meet the public demand for information. What they obtained and passed on to a credulous public was a highly biased and dangerously distorted interpretation of drug addiction.

This book was written to meet the need for an integrated treatment of drug addiction that would embrace all of its multifaceted aspects—pharmacological, psychiatric, psychological, sociological, and educational. Other works directed toward the same purpose are either presently out of date or are oversimplified popularizations of the subject. There are, of course, many excellent technical treatises devoted to single aspects of the subject such as the pharmacological, neurophysiological, or sociological.

The writer has attempted to present, in as nontechnical a style as is compatible with the nature of the literature, a fully documented interpretation of research findings in the field of drug addiction. He hopes that this will prove useful to undergraduate and graduate students in psychology, sociology, and health education, and to all persons whose professional work brings them into contact with drug addicts or with the problem of drug addiction, that is, physicians, psychiatrists, nurses, psychologists, social workers, educators, jurists, and law-enforcement officers. It is also eminently suitable for the well-informed layman interested in public affairs.

For the most part, this book deals with the problem of opiate addiction. The discussion of other drugs such as alcohol, marihuana, the barbiturates, cocaine, the amphetamines, and of some psychotropic drugs used in medicine and psychiatry is intended for comparative purposes only and is not meant to be definitive in nature.

The author obtained firsthand experience with the diagnosis and treatment of drug addiction during 1946 and 1947 in the course of an assignment as medical officer at the U.S. Public Health Service Hospital at Lexington, Kentucky. This volume, however, is based upon a critical and interpretive survey of the literature as well as on personal clinical experience and on clinical and psychometric research at the Lexington hospital. The views expressed in this book are solely the writer's and should not be construed as representing the opinions of any institution with which he is or has been associated.

Portions of this material have already appeared in articles by the writer in the *Psychiatric Quarterly Supplement* and in *Mental Hygiene,* and in a manual on alcohol and narcotic drugs written with Willard B. Spalding for the Office of the Superintendent of Public Instruction of the State of Illinois. The permission to republish excerpts from these works, granted by the above-mentioned publishers, is gratefully acknowledged.

Urbana, Illinois, 1957   David P. Ausubel

Chapter 1
The Problem
of Drug
Addiction*

The Meaning of Drug Addiction

It is necessary at the outset to define what we mean by the terms
drug addiction and *addicting drugs*. According to traditional medical usage, *addiction* refers to a condition brought about by the
repeated administration of any drug "such that continued use of the
drug is necessary to maintain normal physiological function, and
discontinuance of the drug results in definite physical and mental
symptoms" (Isbell, 1951). But usually, when the term *drug addiction* is used without further qualification, addiction to the opiate
group of narcotic drugs is meant.

It has also been customary to distinguish between drugs that are
habit-forming and drugs that are addicting. The former group of
drugs are said to induce "a condition in which the habitué desires a
drug but suffers no ill effects on its discontinuance" (Tatum et al.,
1939). Thus, the drugs in tobacco, coffee, cola drinks, and laxatives
are frequently characterized as habit-forming but not as addicting.

The present writer, however, fails to perceive any value in this
distinction. Physical or psychological habituation, after all, best
describes the condition that develops during the course of drug
addiction and which is responsible for the mental and physical

---

* A glossary of the relatively few, but necessary, technical terms used in this book follows the last
chapter (before the References).

symptoms that arise when the drug is discontinued. Furthermore, many habitual users of tobacco, coffee, alcohol, and laxatives experience profound physical or psychological discomfort when they voluntarily or otherwise forego their usage. Hence, it would be quite correct to use the terms *habit-forming* and *addicting* synonymously and to refer to common habit-forming drugs as addictive in nature.

It is true, however, that although opiates and tobacco are both addicting or habit-forming drugs, addiction to opiates is, in addition, characterized by a phenomenon that does not occur in relation to tobacco or coffee. Habitual usage of an opiate results in physiological changes within the tissues of the body that invariably bring about a stereotyped pattern of physical symptoms when the drug is withdrawn (physical or physiological dependence).

This phenomenon of physical dependence* is responsible for the fact that discontinuance of opiates in addicted persons results in more serious and invariable physical distress than is the case when tobacco or coffee are similarly withdrawn. Furthermore, in the latter instances, since tissue changes are typically not involved, the symptoms of withdrawal are quite variable and are largely or completely absent in many individuals. We can conclude, therefore, that drugs can be habit-forming or addicting even though physical dependence is not involved. But if physical dependence also occurs, the type of addiction that results is characterized by more severe and invariable physical symptoms when the drug is withdrawn.

Thus, when we ask to what drugs one can become addicted, we must include a large number of drugs—stimulants such as cocaine, amphetamines, and mescaline; depressants such as marihuana, opiates, and their derivatives; hypnotics and sedatives such as bromides and barbiturates; and alcohol, tobacco, caffeine, and certain kinds of laxatives. Physical dependence, however, is a relatively rare phenomenon in the total picture of drug addiction. True

---

* Unexplained terms will sometimes appear in the text before they are formally defined. Brief definitions are given in the Glossary, page 144.

Unequivocal evidence of physical dependence exists only for alcohol, barbiturates, "minor" tranquilizers (above a critical dosage level) and, of course, opiates and opiatelike drugs (Cantanzaro, 1971), despite frequent claims to the contrary. And, only in relation to the latter group does a true cellular adaptation mechanism prevail, and is tolerance related to withdrawal and degree of pharmacological effects.

physical dependence probably only develops in relation to opiate and opiatelike drugs, although characteristic withdrawal symptoms are typically found in chronic alcoholism and invariably in advanced cases of barbiturate addiction and addiction to some psychotropic drugs.

Nevertheless, as will be pointed out later, physical dependence is by no means the most important or most dangerous aspect of drug addiction. When it does take place, it merely guarantees the occurrence of a relatively severe and invariable group of withdrawal symptoms. The actual prognosis of a case of drug addiction, however, is primarily a function of psychological and personality factors.

Ways in which Drug Addiction Is Harmful

Drug addiction is merely a *descriptive* term, defining a state of habituation brought about by the continued use of certain drugs. In and of itself, it carries no evaluative connotations. It is harmful or undesirable only if it occurs under conditions which are detrimental to individual or social welfare. Like any other commodity or habit, drugs and habituation to drugs may be used for good or for evil. They can be considered good, bad, or indifferent in value only in terms of their effects. If the compulsive use of various drugs results in unnecessary physical damage, loss of psychological efficiency, perpetuation of immature personality traits, or in social disorganization, addiction is harmful. But contrary to common belief, the mere fact that a drug is habit-forming or is used habitually does not necessarily stamp the drug or the habit as vicious or sinister. This information merely informs us that special care is required in the use of the drug, since the dangers of abuse are naturally enhanced if such abuse may become habitual.

Several examples may help to clarify this point. A great number of individuals who have visual defects, missing teeth, or amputated limbs become habituated to the use of eyeglasses, dentures, or prosthetic devices. Although these artificial aids soon become absolutely essential for adequate vision, chewing, or locomotion, few persons would regard such habituation as harmful.

Similarly, it makes good sense to relieve the pain of incurable cancer with addicting analgesics and to sometimes administer habit-forming hypnotics to certain individuals suffering from chronic insomnia. These latter decisions, naturally, can only be made by competent medical specialists. And insofar as the moderate use of coffee or alcohol has not been demonstrated to be injurious, the addictive aspects of such practices need not be viewed with alarm.*

On the other hand, habituation is harmful and undesirable if it leads unnecessarily to loss of natural functional capacities, if addicting drugs are used for mild and transitory disorders when other less-extreme and nonaddicting remedies would suffice, and, most important, if the effects of such addiction are injurious to the individual or to society. Thus, it is definitely unwise to use routinely, over protracted periods of time, habit-forming laxatives and hypnotics for mild and self-limited cases of constipation and insomnia, respectively. It is obviously even more indefensible to become habituated to drugs that may readily impair physical and mental health or result in widespread social disorganization when no medical indications whatsoever exist for their use.

Need for Social Regulation of Opiate Use

Society's right to suppress opiate addiction is predicated upon two very different kinds of propositions. The first kind of proposition, which merely asserts that such addiction is harmful to both the individual and to society, can be empirically tested. The second kind of proposition, however, is based entirely on a philosophy of law or government and cannot be either proven or disproven. This latter proposition rests on the assumption that society may invade the domain of personal rights both to protect the general welfare and to prevent the individual from knowingly or unknowingly inflicting harm upon himself. Although unprovable, this latter proposition is so firmly embedded in our entire legal system and structure of government that it requires no further justification.

Interestingly enough, the drug addict generally tends to reject both sets of propositions. In the same breath, he denies that opiate addiction is injurious to the individual or to the social order, and belligerently asserts that, even if it were, an individual's vices are his

---

* This statement is only meant to reflect a medical and psychological value judgment. The writer does not presume to judge the moral, religious, legal, or political issues involved in such questions as abstinence and prohibition.

own private affair. According to him, opiates are no more of a social menace than alcohol or tobacco. Hence, he sees no reason why he should be forbidden the enjoyment of his special brand of drug pleasure when other persons are at liberty to do as they please with respect to their drugs.

He often maintains that if he were assured a steady supply of drugs and could be spared the time, effort, and concern that normally go into their acquisition, he would experience no difficulty in holding down a job and would even work more effectively under their influence. He proudly points to the alleged existence of a group of brilliant men who are addicts unknown to society and maintain themselves on small daily doses. Finally, he claims that restrictive narcotic laws have caused more addiction than any other single factor.

What are the facts in the case? In the first place, it has been unequivocally established by systematic observation under controlled conditions that when an addict is permitted to use as much of a narcotic drug as he wants, he characteristically becomes lethargic, slovenly, undependable, and devoid of ambition (Wikler, 1953). The drug-satiated addict loses all desire for socially productive work and exhibits little interest in food, sex, companionship, family ties, or recreation. The so-called "push" which he attributes to the influence of the drug becomes evident only when he becomes concerned about the source of his next dose.

The addict's belief that he can work more efficiently under the influence of drugs is merely an illusion created by the euphoria he experiences with drug usage. Objective tests actually demonstrate deceleration in speed of tapping and learning and in verbal- and motor-reaction time. The typical addict uses as high a dose of the drug as he can afford or obtain, and almost invariably more than he requires to remain free of the uncomfortable symptoms he experiences upon withdrawal of the drug (Kolb and Himmelsbach, 1938). "Hence the brilliant surgeon or philosopher addict who limits himself to a small dose to 'steady his nerves' or 'sharpen his mental faculties' is mostly a myth" (Ausubel, 1948).

These pernicious effects of narcotic addiction on individual productivity are hardly surprising in view of the known adjustive properties of opiates for addiction-prone individuals. If "the goal of personal satisfaction" normally achieved through socially valuable activities directed toward "security, prestige, family attachments, financial independence . . . can be acquired through the simple expedient of injecting morphine, these activities are rendered superfluous, and the addict becomes a useless burden on his family and society in general" (Wikler, 1944). Primarily for this reason, society, for its own protection, is required to legislate against drug addiction. "Easy availability would lead to . . . use by thousands or perhaps hundreds of thousands of neurotic, psychopathic or otherwise inadequate people of whom there are plenty in society" (Wikler, 1944).

> In times of social demoralization, the habit, because of its efficient adjustive value, would be acquired by a large segment of the population; and as shown by historical experience in China and Egypt would be a major contributing factor toward perpetuating poverty, ignorance, and lack of social and economic progress (Ausubel, 1948).

Although the writer certainly holds no brief for the intemperate use of alcohol, it is important to recognize that alcohol is a decidedly less dangerous drug. It does not generate sufficient euphoria and its adjustive value is insufficient to serve as a complete and satisfactory substitute for all productive human activity. The acquisition of genuine tolerance to the effects of alcohol occurs almost universally, but is extremely variable. Over the course of continued use it may either increase or decrease.*

It is also true that alcoholism is currently responsible for more illness, death, crime, and social disorganization than is opiate addiction; but it must be remembered that the number of persons knowingly exposed to narcotics is very much smaller compared to the number of persons using alcoholic beverages. In any event, the evils associated with excessive use of alcohol provide more of an argument for the control of such abuses than they provide justification for the elimination of narcotic controls or the legalization of marihuana. Despite the addict's statement to the contrary, law enforcement has materially reduced the incidence of drug addiction.

---

* Unlike the case of opiates, tolerance is not necessarily related to physical dependence; hence, increases or decreases in tolerance are generally unrelated either to changes in physical dependence or in the physical and behavioral effects of the drug. Further, the underlying mechanisms of physical dependence in alcohol and opiates respectively are undoubtedly different (see chapter 2).

The illegality of drug addiction has incentive value per se only to the aggressive, antisocial psychopath and to the thrill-seeking adolescent.

It has been convincingly argued that drug addiction, like alcoholism, is a disease requiring treatment rather than a crime requiring punishment. As will be pointed out later, this proposition certainly has considerable merit. It is, at any rate, difficult to appreciate the logic or consistency of regarding the chronic alcoholic as an ill person and the drug addict as a criminal.

There is a marked difference, however, between not regarding drug addiction as a crime and legalizing the practice, that is, allowing everyone free access to the drug. The suggestion advanced by certain well-intentioned but misinformed persons that the habit be legalized for present known addicts only is unsatisfactory, because it would provide legal and moral sanction for the habit and thus encourage its spread, without in any way eradicating the illicit market in drugs.

Chapter 2
Physiological and Psychological Effects of Opiate Drugs

Before the nature of drug addiction can be genuinely understood, some knowledge of the effects of narcotic drugs on the human body is necessary. Without such knowledge, it would be impossible to explain how and why addiction takes place in predisposed persons, or why narcotic drugs have more adjustive value to these persons than sodium bicarbonate or milk of magnesia.

By definition, a narcotic drug is one that induces sleep and stupor and relieves pain. Strictly speaking, therefore, alcohol, marihuana, the barbiturates, ether, chloroform, and nitrous oxide would have to be classified as narcotics. This discussion, however, will only deal with opiates and opiatelike drugs.

Types Used by Addicts

Crude opium is the juice of the incised, unripe seed capsules of the opium poppy, *Papaver somniferum* (Goodman and Gilman, 1970). The opium poppy requires a hot, dry climate and very careful cultivation. Because the yield per acre is small and because laborious care is required in collecting the juice, it can only be grown profitably where both land and labor are cheap, for example, in Turkey, Iran, and India. When prepared (purified), opium can be eaten or smoked. The eating and smoking of opium, however, are rare today except in the Far East. Alcoholic extracts of opium are still used medically and also occasionally by drug addicts.

9

The pharmacologically active principals in opium are *alkaloids,* the two most important of which are *morphine* and *codeine.* Both are addicting and analgesic drugs, but morphine is much more potent. It was until the fifties the most commonly used drug in the United States for addiction purposes, except in the East, where heroin use was typical (Meyer, 1952). Morphine was also the drug of choice among women addicts in the past and still is among addicts drawn from the medical profession and from the upper socioeconomic strata. Experimentation with different kinds of opiates, however, is quite common, especially among men addicts. Morphine is generally injected either subcutaneously or intravenously (mainline). The latter method is more frequently used by men and by inveterate addicts.

*Heroin** (diacetylmorphine) is a semisynthetic derivative of morphine which has very similar properties but is more potent. Because it induces more euphoria than morphine, it is correspondingly more addicting; and since it is not required medically, its manufacture in or importation to the United States has been made illegal. The heroin which is used so extensively by addicts on the East Coast is smuggled into this country from Italy, France, Germany, Mexico, and the Near and Far East. Heroin addicts usually begin by sniffing the powder nasally and then graduate to subcutaneous and intravenous techniques. Another semisynthetic derivative of morphine, *dilaudid,* is therapeutically active in doses about one-fourth that of morphine and is correspondingly more toxic (Goodman and Gilman, 1970).

Within the past forty years, pharmacologists have discovered how to make potent, opiatelike analgesics synthetically without starting from opium or its derivatives. Two of these drugs, *meperidine (Demerol®)* and *methadone (Dolophine®)* are already in common medical use and are also used by addicts. Demerol® is much less analgesic than morphine but also produces less euphoria and very little hypnosis; its effects are relatively short-lasting. Methadone is notable for its marked and prolonged hypnotic effects and for the long duration of its analgesia and euphoria (Wikler, 1953). It gives

---

* It is ironic that heroin was originally introduced in the United States as a means of treating morphine addiction.

rise to a less severe but longer-lasting abstinence syndrome when withdrawn than does heroin.

Wide variability exists with respect to the daily dosage of drugs taken by individual addicts. The actual amounts addicts report using must be accepted with caution because of differences in the extent to which the drug is adulterated (cut) before it is sold by peddlers. Furthermore, when apprehended, addicts tend to exaggerate their customary dosage in hopes of receiving larger doses during the course of withdrawal treatment. The median daily dose reported in most studies varies between the equivalent of five and twelve grains of morphine and in any case is considerably greater than the amount required to prevent withdrawal symptoms. It is estimated that 57 percent of drug abusers are currently involved in multiple-drug use.*

General Effects on the Human Body

Opiates act chiefly on the central and autonomic nervous systems and, to some extent, directly on smooth muscle. Effects on the central nervous system are primarily depressant, although larger doses may bring out stimulant properties, especially at the spinal level of reaction. In general, "morphine depresses from above downward; and stimulates from below upward" (Goodman and Gilman, 1970). "Nevertheless, specific stimulant actions," even with analgesic doses, "occur at all anatomic levels of integration," sometimes following initial depression (Wikler, 1953). The depressant actions include analgesia (relief of pain), sedation (freedom from anxiety, muscular relaxation, decreased motor activity), hypnosis (drowsiness and lethargy), and euphoria (a sense of well-being and contentment).

The characteristic and most useful property of opiates as central nervous system depressants is their ability (unlike anesthetics) to produce marked analgesia without excessive drowsiness, muscular weakness, confusion, or loss of consciousness. By the same token, however, and also because they selectively depress the respiratory

---

* As the use of heroin has decreased in recent years because of the decreased production in Turkey and increased adulteration of the drug, the illicit use of methadone has correspondingly increased. This is the case because methadone is cheaper, can be purchased from licit users of the drug, is effective orally, and is longer-lasting in its effects. *New York Times*, July 6, 1975. (Report of White House Special Action Office for Drug Abuse Prevention.)

center, they cannot be used effectively for anesthetic purposes. The autonomic nervous system effects (direct or mediated through the central nervous system) include constriction of the pupil, slowing of the pulse rate, vomiting, and flushing of the skin. Opiates generally increase the tonus of smooth muscle but inhibit peristalsis. In the intestinal tract, this leads to constipation.

Exactly how opiates induce analgesia is not completely understood. It is quite certain, however, that more than one mechanism is involved. In the first place, by depressing the cerebral cortex, they typically, but not always, elevate the threshold for pain perception (Wolff et al., 1940). (Since a decorticate animal [an animal without a cerebral cortex] has a higher pain threshold than an intact animal, it follows that the cortex must lower the threshold for pain perception.)

Second, by virtue of their depressant action on the cortex, opiates raise the threshold for the perception of threatening stimuli such as pain,* thereby reducing the anticipatory anxiety associated with it (Wikler, 1953). "The pain is still perceived but it no longer brings forth the usual [emotional] responses. The patient is capable of tolerating the experience of pain when it is freed of its [threatening] implications" (Ausubel, 1948).

Third, opiates are analgesic because of their hypnotic properties, "sleep in itself raising the threshold for pain by approximately fifty percent" (Wolff et al., 1940).

Finally, but perhaps most important, the analgesia induced by opiates seems to be intimately identified with the psychological experience of euphoria (Ausubel, 1948; Seevers in the Committee on Public Health Relations of the New York Academy of Medicine's *Conference on Drug Addiction Among Adolescents*, 1953). This action is very similar to the effect of interrupting the

---

* However, the cortex simultaneously inhibits the motor response to the perception of threat inherent in pain. Thus, a decorticate animal shows a greater motor response to pain than an intact animal. Also, overreaction to pain (and pleasure) occurs in the thalamic syndrome of Dejerine and Roussy, in which the thalamus is released from the restraining influence which the cortex exerts through the cortico-thalamic fibers (the tract connecting the cortex to the thalamus). Hence, as a result of cortical and cortico-thalamic inhibition, morphine should increase the motor response to pain. But since it actually does the opposite, even depressing the motor components of sham rage in a decorticate animal, a direct subcortical action in the opposite direction must predominate.

thalamo-cortical tract,* performed in prefrontal lobotomy.† As a result of the inhibition of the self-critical faculty, the previously unbearable pain is still perceived but is ignored by the patient as inconsequential. This effect may account in part for the diminished emotional reaction to pain despite the cortical and cortico-thalamic depressant actions of morphine which would otherwise tend to enhance the motor and emotional response to pain.

It is evident, therefore, that analgesia and euphoria are closely related, and that the pain-reducing properties of a drug are to a great extent dependent upon its ability to produce euphoria (inhibition of the self-critical faculty) (Ausubel, 1948). Since it is the euphoria-producing properties of a drug that are primarily responsible for its addicting potential, it seems inevitable that all potent analgesics must simultaneously be addicting. Thus the hope of preventing addiction by synthesizing a satisfactory nonaddicting analgesic—a task that has engaged the efforts of our best pharmacologists for over forty years—seems forlorn indeed.‡ This prediction made 28 years ago by the writer (Ausubel, 1948), was virtually conceded by a leading pharmacologist in 1953 (M.H. Seevers, in *Conference on Drug Addiction Among Adolescents*).

This, of course, does not mean that the analgesic action of a drug cannot be separated from other noneuphoric properties frequently associated with it. Analgesics such as the salicylates have relatively weak sedative properties, and the strongly sedative barbiturates are only mildly analgesic. The spinal stimulant properties of opiates, and even their autonomic effects, can be separated from their analgesic properties. The latter separation theoretically makes possible the synthesis of a potent analgesic which leads to only a

---

* The identification by the writer of the thalamo-cortical tract as the gross neuroanatomical site of the euphoric action of opiates is not accepted by all authorities in the field even though it is consistent with the effects of prefrontal lobotomy and of spontaneous lesions in this tract. Focal electrical stimulation of the rat brain results in analgesia to which gradual tolerance is acquired. Addiction to morphine greatly reduces this electrically stimulated tolerance, thereby demonstrated cross-tolerance between the two methods of inducing analgesia. (D. H. Mayer and R. H. Hayes, "Stimulation-produced analgesia: Development of tolerance and cross-tolerance to morphine." *Science*, May 30,1975)

† This is a brain operation that was once frequently performed to treat severely depressed mental patients obsessed by guilt feelings and patients suffering from intractable pain.

‡ Recent narcotic antagonists, such as cyclazocine, however, seem to be nonaddicting, noneuphorogenous analgesics and, partly for this reason, have been used in treating narcotic addicts (Jaffe, 1970; Chappel et al, 1971).

minimal degree of physical dependence. In part, this probably accounts for the relatively mild abstinence syndrome (with only few autonomic symptoms) following methadone withdrawal in man. However, as will be pointed out later, physical dependence plays only a minor role in the causation of opiate addiction. Hence, the discovery of such an analgesic will have little effect on the incidence of drug addiction as long as it necessarily induces euphoria at the very same time.

Properties Related to Addiction

Three pharmacological properties of the opiates are especially related to their addictive propensities—tolerance, physiological dependence, and euphoria. The physiological mechanisms underlying these phenomena have not yet been definitely established. Hence, we can present below only the most cogent of present-day thinking. Since tolerance and physiological dependence are so closely related, it will be convenient to consider them together.

Tolerance

Tolerance refers to a progressive increase in the ability of the body to adapt to the effects of a drug that is used at regular and frequent intervals. It is manifested in two ways: (1) progressively larger doses must be administered to produce the same effects; and (2) eventually as much as ten or more times the original lethal dose can safely be taken. In the case of the opiates, tolerance to the various effects of the drug is not uniformly acquired. It is hardly ever acquired for the tonic effects of opiates on smooth muscle (for example, constipation) (Goodman and Gilman, 1970); and it is acquired relatively slowly for the analgesic and pupil-narrowing effects of the drug. Hence,

> one can keep patients free of pain for months on the same small dose. On the other hand, tolerance is developed very quickly for the euphoric action of morphine. To keep on getting the same "kick" out of the drug, dosage must be quickly raised to a very high level (Ausubel, 1952).

The latter result can also be largely achieved with a stabilized dose providing that it is administered intravenously.

Though not accepted by all pharmacologists, the most satisfactory and parsimonious explanation of tolerance,* which simultaneously explains the related phenomenon of physical dependence, is that it is reflective of an adaptive increase in the responsiveness of certain cells of the body to their normal regulatory influences.

All orderly bodily functions are maintained and regulated by a system of internal stimuli, i.e., by hormones, enzymes, vitamins, and nerve impulses. A drug such as morphine produces various effects on the body because it interferes with or opposes the normal operation of these regulatory influences. If, however, the drug is taken over a period of time, the body tissues learn to *adapt*—that is, to become more sensitive—to the internal stimuli that govern them. Thus, these tissues become able to function adequately even though the greater part of their normal physiological stimulation is counteracted by the drug.

Here is where *physiological dependence* enters the picture. Suppose we suddenly withdraw the drug. The normal physiological stimulus can now operate unopposed, in full force. But in the process of adapting to morphine, the tissues have become *supersensitive* to the action of this internal stimulus that morphine opposes. Hence, this normal level of the internal stimulus will now act as an *overdose* and cause unpleasant [abstinence] symptoms. To avoid them, the addicted individual need only take morphine again. Thus, he becomes physiologically dependent on the drug in the sense that he must use it habitually to prevent the onset of physiological distress (Ausubel, 1952).

Two other mechanisms, which are in no sense incompatible with the cellular adaptation theory, probably play a subsidiary role in the development of tolerance and/or physical dependence. First, in the course of acquiring tolerance, it has been shown that the addict develops increased ability to destroy or alter opiates, as indicated by the greater percentage of morphine that can be recovered from the urine of nontolerant individuals. And, second, pointing to the known excitant effects of morphine (especially at the spinal level of reaction) which occur simultaneously with and apparently outlast the depressant effects, Tatum, Seevers, and Collins (1929) suggest that a cumulative state of masked excitation is established after successive injections of the drug. These authors hypothesize that this state of masked hypersensitivity may counteract the current depressant effects of later injections and may be released

---

* Cross-tolerance also exists among the opiate and opiatelike drugs, that is, tolerance acquired to one is acquired, in part, to all; and *any* one can relieve the abstinence symptoms caused by the withdrawal of another.

(unmasked) by abrupt withdrawal of the drug, thereby precipitating the abstinence syndrome.

Wikler (1953) proposes a very similar explanation, stating that the "morphine abstinence syndrome may be due to 'excitant' actions of morphine which are 'masked' by its 'depressant' actions." He states, however, that the excitant effects (which morphine induces simultaneously with the depressant effects on the same or related functions) may be released prior to the development of tolerance and, therefore, that "the mechanisms related to tolerance may be independent of those related to the morphine abstinence syndrome." More recently, Wikler (1977) has attributed withdrawal symptoms in detoxified addicts to "conditioning phenomena to environmental cues."

Abstinence

The abstinence syndrome itself naturally represents *antagonistic* responses to the effects of morphine in the three major groups of tissues influenced by the drug. These withdrawal symptoms consist of yawning, sneezing, tearing of the eyes, a running nose, goose flesh, rapid pulse, increased blood pressure, dilated pupils, hot and cold flashes, nausea, vomiting, diarrhea, loss of appetite, weight loss, muscular twitches, and, sometimes, sexual orgasm. Objective laboratory signs include elevations in blood sugar, white blood cell count, and body temperature. The patient complains of restlessness, intense craving for opiates, insomnia, and various aches and pains. He is anxious, irritable, and irascibly demanding of drugs.*

Although these symptoms are undoubtedly uncomfortable, they are seldom more severe than a bad case of gastrointestinal influenza. They endanger life only if the addicted individual is old and feeble or is suffering from cardiac disease. Furthermore,

> the condition is a self-limited one which disappears in about ten days. Hence it can be safely concluded that few persons ever become

---

* Infants of addicted mothers also exhibit abstinence symptoms at birth by virtue of becoming physiologically dependent on narcotics reaching them from the maternal bloodstream through the placenta. Some of the symptoms of addicted newborn infants include a continuous high-pitched cry; reduction in sucking rate, pressure, and amount consumed; and below-average height and weight.

addicted because they are dependent upon the drug to avoid withdrawal symptoms (Ausubel, 1948).

All opiatelike drugs induce euphoria and are able to relieve or
prevent the onset of withdrawal symptoms. They differ quantita-
tively among themselves, however, with respect to the development
of tolerance and physical dependence. The abstinence syndrome
following methadone, for example, is relatively mild and prolonged
in comparison to that of morphine and heroin, and includes only a
minimum of autonomic symptoms (Wikler, 1953). For this reason,
it is the drug of choice in the treatment of the heroin or morphine
abstinence syndromes. The abstinence syndromes following heroin
and dilaudid are severe but of short duration, whereas that of
meperidine (Demerol®) is much less intense.

To reach the stage of intracellular adaptation (tolerance) such
that abrupt withdrawal of the drug results in abstinence symptoms
(physiological dependence) typically requires the regular administration of several injections daily over a period of two or more weeks
(Jaffe, 1970). This interval varies depending on the drug used, the
dosage, the timing between doses, the method of administration, and
on physical and psychological differences among individual users.
Definite and progressively more severe abstinence symptoms appear
about 12 hours after abrupt withdrawal of the drug, reach a peak
within 48 to 72 hours, and "subside gradually over a period of about
one week. Some physiologic variables, however, do not return to
control levels for as long as six months" (Wikler, 1953). The
severity of the symptoms depends on the same factors listed above,
plus the "duration of addiction and the degree of tolerance which
had been developed" (Wikler, 1953). The most probable explanation for the unique development of marked physiological
dependence in the case of the opiate drugs lies both in the unusual
degree of tolerance that can be developed in relation to them and in
the multiplicity of their central nervous system, and autonomic and
smooth muscle actions.

Good reasons exist for believing that the abstinence syndrome is
in part conditioned by personality and situational factors. Marked
individual differences in severity and types of symptoms occur
among addicts "accustomed to similar dose levels of morphine over
comparable lengths of time" (Wikler, 1953). Symptoms also vary

depending upon the individual's past addiction experience, his expectations of what is going to happen, his current needs, and the attitudes of associates and attending physicians. Such evidence, however, does not disprove the physical basis of withdrawal illness. It merely indicates that the behavioral manifestations of this condition are also influenced by psychological factors. No other conclusion is possible when we consider that the same symptoms appear in similar progression in addicted chimpanzees, monkeys, and dogs, even when the cerebral cortex of the latter animal is removed (Seevers,* 1953; Spragg, 1940; Wikler, 1950, 1953); that it is very unlikely that psychological factors alone could produce the objective laboratory signs listed above; and that withdrawal symptoms are unaffected by placebos, nonopiate sedatives, and hypnosis.

In summary, therefore, three different mechanisms may possibly account for the development of tolerance and physical dependence:

(1) A state of adaptive hypersensitivity of nerve and smooth muscle cells to their normal regulatory influences which develops in the course of acquiring tolerance to morphine.

(2) Residual but masked excitant effects of morphine which when cumulated may both provide some tolerance to the drug and result in abstinence symptoms when it is abruptly withdrawn. This cumulative state of central excitation, masked by the depressant effects of the current dose of morphine, is, of course, in no way comparable to the adaptive cellular hypersensitivity described above. It apparently builds up quickly enough so that it can be released even prior to the development of tolerance,† although it is naturally more intense after tolerance has been acquired. We are evidently dealing here with earlier and later stages of the *same* mechanism and not with a separate mechanism for tolerance and for physical dependence.

---

* In Committee on Public Relations of the New York Academy of Medicine, *Conference on Drug Addiction Among Adolescents.* New York: Blariston 1953.

† Abstinence symptoms cannot be demonstrated clinically by abrupt withdrawal of the drug prior to the development of tolerance. But in both animals and man, N-allylnormorphine (which when administered after morphine antagonizes its depressant effects) can precipitate withdrawal signs after relatively few small doses of morphine. In chronic spinal dogs this occurs even after single doses of morphine (Wikler, 1953).

(3) An adaptive ability exists to destroy or deactivate the drug more effectively in the course of its intermediate metabolism, which develops after successive injections.

The weight of the evidence indicates, however, that adaptive cellular hypersensitivity is probably the centrally important mechanism involved in the development of both tolerance and physical dependence. More rapid deactivation may account for some of the tolerance; and cumulative masked excitation may account for both some tolerance and part of the post-tolerance abstinence syndrome under clinical conditions of withdrawal. Nevertheless, it is evident that abstinencelike signs may be precipitated pharmacologically before tolerance is acquired.

Physiological Dependence

The role of physiological (physical) dependence in causing addiction has been both minimized and exaggerated. That this phenomenon exists and is basically responsible for the general features of the abstinence syndrome (if not for specific elaboration influenced by personality and situational factors) is undeniable. It is also clear that, once addicted, the prevention of withdrawal symptoms constitutes *one* of the addict's motivations for continued use of the drug. Clinical evidence also indicates that this distress-relieving potential of the drug enhances its euphoric properties (Wikler, 1953). Furthermore, psychologically normal individuals receiving opiates for therapeutic purposes over long periods of time occasionally do experience difficulty in terminating their addiction because of physical dependence. After withdrawal is accomplished, however, such persons usually do not revert to the use of drugs.

But even apart from the fact that the abstinence syndrome is neither catastrophically severe nor long-lasting, there are many reasons for believing that physiological dependence does not play a central cause-effect role in drug addiction. The popular misconceptions that addicted individuals deprived of the drug suffer the tortures of the damned, and that once caught in the iron grip of physiological dependence the average person is powerless to help himself, are beliefs that have been foisted on a credulous public by misinformed journalists and by addicts themselves.

In the first place, unless other subjective satisfactions were derived from the habit, it is difficult to believe that any individual would be willing to pay the fantastic price of the drug and risk imprisonment, social disgrace, and ostracism merely to avoid a moderately severe ten-day illness.

Second, it is well known to most practicing physicians that every year thousands of patients suffering from protractedly painful illness receive opiates regularly over sufficiently prolonged periods of time to develop marked physical dependence on the drug. Nevertheless, despite frequent awareness of this state of affairs, the vast majority of such patients are able to terminate their dependence quite easily following gradual reduction of dosage. Unlike addicts, they do not claim that they are compelled to continue using the drug because of the intolerability of the abstinence symptoms.

Third, the amount of morphine required to prevent withdrawal symptoms is characteristically no more than one-half to one-tenth the actual dosage used by most addicts. How, therefore, can one account for this surplus dosage if the drug is merely taken, as some addicts claim, "just to stay normal"?

Fourth, abstinence symptoms can be adequately relieved when either morphine, heroin, or methadone is injected hypodermically. Hence, why will addicts run the added risk of thrombophlebitis, septicemia, and hepatitis, by injecting the drug "mainline" (intravenously) with crude, homemade syringes? The answer to both of these questions is that the excessive dose and the "mainline" route increase the "kick" or the euphoric effect of the drug.

Fifth, the synthetic opiate, methadone, which has all of the analgesic and euphoric properties of morphine and heroin leads to withdrawal symptoms that are relatively milder, though more long-lasting. Nevertheless, the evidence is conclusive that addiction develops about as rapidly for this drug as for other opiates.

Finally, if physiological dependence were the primary causative factor in perpetuating the drug habit, how could one explain the fact that at least 90 percent of the drug addicts discharged from federal hospitals start using the drug again almost immediately after release? By this time, it is usually at least a year since their physical dependence was broken. If they really find withdrawal symptoms tolerable only by surrendering to chronic addiction, why should they start all over again when they obviously do not have to? We can only assume that various positive and pleasureable gratifications are associated with the practice, among which is the satisfying experience of alleviating the distress of withdrawal symptoms. In this latter connection, it seems fair to conclude that physiological dependence primarily contributes to the original addiction process, and to the later relapse, not by generating an undeniable need for relieving or circumventing physical suffering as an end in itself, but by enhancing the euphoric action of opiates.

Euphoria

If physiological dependence cannot satisfactorily account for the causation of drug addiction, what else does? The most credible answer we can offer in the present state of medical knowledge is that opiates owe their marked addicting properties to the feelings of euphoria which they engender. These euphoric attributes of the drug have unusual adjustive value for individuals with certain kinds of personality makeup. Naturally, not all persons so predisposed become drug addicts. The drug must first be available. Much also depends on the immediate social milieu and the wider cultural environment of the addiction-prone individual.

Euphoria is usually defined as a generalized feeling of well-being in the absence of any objective justification for such a feeling. Most commonly, as for example in manic states, this condition is a reflection of an impaired self-critical ability. It can also be enhanced by intense pleasurable feelings and by an absence of pain (or an inability to respond to painful, disagreeable stimuli). Opiates induce euphoria in all three ways. Much of their analgesic value is attributable to their ability to elevate the perceptual threshold for pain, to inhibit the anticipatory anxiety associated with pain, and to minimize the seriousness to self with which pain is regarded (impairment of self-critical faculty). After an intravenous injection of morphine, addicts "report that they feel 'fixed.' This term appears to denote a state of gratification and well-being in which hunger, pain and sexual urges are greatly reduced or abolished" (Wikler, 1953). In addition, injection of morphine results in a highly pleasurable thrill or "rush" which is "described as similar to orgasm except that the sensation seems to be centered in the abdomen" (Wikler, 1953).*

It is important to note that tolerance to the euphoric action of the opiates is quickly acquired. Thereafter, to continue obtaining this effect, the addict must increase the dosage of the drug or "mainline it." The euphoria can also be enhanced by postponing injection until mild abstinence changes occur (Wikler, 1953). Hence, although the euphoria of the later stages is probably less intense than at the onset of addiction, it can still be experienced by resorting to these devices.

It is also important to realize that euphoria is not an invariable concomitant of opiate use. Initially, before tolerance is acquired, opiates result in such disagreeable symptoms as nausea, vomiting, anxiety, and depression (Jaffe, 1970; Zimmering, 1951). Furthermore, some addicts, especially those with essentially normal personalities who are accidentally addicted, experience no euphoria at all or at most a very mild degree of it. Even inveterate "mainliners" sometimes fail to derive any pleasure from the drug under inauspicious circumstances (for example, when experiencing fear, distrust, suspicion) (Wikler, 1953). Exceptions such as these, however, hardly negate the general rule, even when bolstered by the steadfast assertions of most addicts that they do not experience any euphoria from the drug and use it just to stay normal.†

How are such assertions to be evaluated? Lindesmith (1947) and other sociologists who have little experience with the pharmacology of opiates, with the experimental addiction of human subjects, and with the clinical course of addiction tend to accept the addict's statement at face value. They ignore the fact that addicts are both highly motivated to rationalize the basis of their addiction and do not enjoy high reputations for sincerity or insight. They also ignore the six considerations listed above (see pp. 20-21), which challenge the credibility of physiological dependence as a satisfactory theory of addiction.

---

* Apart from the direct pleasurable effects of the thrill, morphine may produce euphoria by causing an overreaction to pleasure through cortical and cortico-thalamic inhibition. Decorticate but not decerebrate animals are capable of experiencing pleasure.

† In recent years, however, the majority of addicts admit that they experience euphoria from heroin (i.e., they continue using it because they enjoy the high).

Much more convincing than the denial of many addicts (who have good reason to disclaim any euphoria) is the evidence, already cited, obtained under controlled conditions of experimental readdiction (Wikler, 1952). This is supported by the frank admission by many hospitalized addict patients (Ausubel, 1948; Zimmering, 1951) that they customarily take two shots, one to prevent withdrawal, the other for the kick. When the role of euphoria in the analgesic action of opiates and the general tendency for addicts to increase their dosage and to use the drug intravenously are added to such evidence, the conclusion is inescapable that, under ordinary conditions of addiction, the typical drug addict experiences euphoria in drug use.*

---

* The recent discovery of a pituitary opioid hormone (endorphin), which pharmacologically resembles opium in terms of locus and type of action on the nervous system, both confirms and expands some of these speculations regarding the relationships between analgesia, euphoria, and prefrontal lobotomy. Similar opioid substances, called *enkephalins,* are also produced by brain tissue itself in the pituitary area.

It seems highly probable that this hormone is responsible for the normal euphoria of most young persons, before middle age sets in, i.e., perceiving themselves, their abilities, and their prospects somewhat more optimistically than a realistic estimate of the same would warrant. (In this sense, internally produced opiate hormones have adaptive or survival values for the individual as well as the species, by increasing persistence or frustration tolerance. As such they probably play a role in biological evolution.) Stretching the analogy one step further, one might hypothesize that mania, on the other hand, is the outcome of an overproduction of this hormone and that depression, on the other, is a reflection of functionally reduced levels of the hormone, in both instances operating on the thalamo-cortical tract. This hypothesis would be an alternative to the catecholamine hypothesis, which holds that increased or decreased levels of central neurotransmitter brain amines at certain synaptic junctions are the principal factor in causing these two disorders, respectively.

This latter possibility, of course, does not rule out the operation of such psychogenic factors as reduced or increased levels of self-criticism and catastrophic degrees of neurotic anxiety. In this instance, increased secretion of the pituitary opioid hormone would merely *mediate* the effects of drastically changed levels of self-criticism and self-esteem, by depressing the thalamo-cortical tract. For recent overviews of the literature on the pituitary opioid hormone, see R. Restak, "The Brain Makes Its Own Narcotics," *Saturday Review,* March 5, 1977, pp. 7-11; A. Goldstein, "Opioid Peptides (endorphins) in Pituitary and Brain," *Science* 193, No. 4258, September 17, 1976, pp. 1081-86; S. H. Snyder, "Opiate Receptors in the Brain," *New England Journal of Medicine* 296, February 3, 1977, pp. 267-71.

The reasons for believing that opiates primarily cause euphoria (and analgesia) by depressing the thalamo-cortical and/or cortico-thalamic tracts are that (a) a prefrontal lobotomy severing these tracts relieves obsessive guilt feelings, depression, and intractable pain; and (b) spontaneous lesions of this tract (Dejerine's syndrome) result in an overreaction to pleasurable stimuli. Thus, in a sense, opiate administration constitutes a pharmacological substitute for prefrontal lobotomy. The identification of the gross neural locus of opiate action is, of course, in no sense incompatible with receptor sites (microscopic) on molecular membranes. (See S. H. Snyder, "Opiate Receptors and Internal Opiates," *Scientific American,* March 1977, pp. 44-56.)

One may also speculate that endorphins and enkephalins enable most people to respond with equanimity to the threat of total extinction posed by the inevitability of death.

Recognition of the Drug Addict

Recognition of the drug addict, especially when he is obtaining his customary dosage, is extremely difficult. Few addicts are willing to reveal their condition, and long experience makes them very adept at disguising it. "Physical findings in opiate addicts are generally not outstanding and never diagnostic" (Isbell, 1951). Positive identification can only be made by laboratory examination. Even withdrawal symptoms, although highly suggestive, are in no sense specific, and therefore are not conclusive. For these reasons, recognition should only be attempted under hospital conditions, that is, in a drug-free environment allowing for prolonged observation and for physical and laboratory examination.

The first few injections of opiates may result in nausea, vomiting, and intense itching. Unaccountable possession of a needle and syringe, of sniffing cones, or of a bent, blackened spoon and homemade eyedropper syringe is suspicious and perhaps the only indication of early drug use. After physical dependence sets in, other signs appear. Needle marks, scars and abscesses on the arm and forearm, and tattooing, fibrosis, and hardening of the superficial veins are extremely suggestive but must be differentiated from other injuries, insect bites, and evidence of legitimate hypodermic injections (for example, in diabetics). Before much tolerance is developed, the pupils may be pinpoint in size. Afterwards, pupillary constriction may be only minimal, and in any event is replaced by dilatation in the early stages of withdrawal. Long-standing addicts tend to be pale and emaciated, and to suffer from severe constipation. Their appetites are poor, and they show little or no sex interest.* Insufficient menstrual bleeding and other menstrual disorders are common.†

Various behavioral changes are also characteristic of advanced addiction. The opiate addict, when his drug supply is assured, is typically in a lethargic, semistuporous, and dreamy state.‡ He is

---

* Premature ejaculation, retarded ejaculation and impotence are very common in drug-free addicts. It is unclear, however, whether these disorders antedate or accompany narcotic addiction or are "subtle abstinence reactions." (Mintz, et al., 1974)

† Santen, et al., attribute these disorders to morphine's action on the central nervous system which in turn reduces the blood level of pituitary gonadotropins, especially estrogens (resulting in amenorrhoea), and in oligo-ovulation, causing irregular menses.

‡ *Nodding* is the addict slang for this condition.

subdued, unaggressive, and withdrawn, and shows little interest in his appearance and surroundings. His preoccupation with obtaining drugs interferes with his normal educational or vocational pursuits. Lying, theft, dissimulation, and importunate demands on others are almost inevitable concomitants of addiction, and reflect the addict's desperate craving for drugs in the face of social and legal condemnation. Few addicts admit to any remorse for stealing to support their habits.

If the physically dependent addict can be detained for more than twelve hours, the appearance of withdrawal symptoms, which grow progressively more severe, materially aids the diagnosis. Some of these same symptoms, however, are also found in hay fever, colds, influenza, and gastrointestinal influenza.

Hence, unless the entire constellation of characteristic symptoms, including dilated pupils, rapid pulse, elevated blood pressure, goose flesh, needle marks, and a history of addiction, is present, diagnostic caution is indicated. Such antiopiates as N-allylnormorphine and naloxone are useful for diagnostic purposes since they can precipitate a full-blown abstinence syndrome almost immediately after injection. Traces of morphine can be detected in the urine as long as ten days after the last injection of heroin.

Relation of Addiction to Physical and Mental Disease

Very little evidence is available to indicate that drug addiction per se is significantly related to physical or mental disease. The harmful results of drug addiction are not due to the toxic effects of opiates on any bodily tissue, fluid, or function, but to their effects on personality and behavior.

Exhaustive medical and laboratory tests fail to reveal any very significant differences between opiate addicts and nonaddicts. The only abnormality that can be definitely attributed to the pharmacological action of the drug is a severe constipation alternating with diarrhea, and not infrequent menstrual problems in women (Santen et al, 1975). All of the other characteristic ailments of the addict are secondary in nature. Loss of appetite, weight loss, malnutrition (and the resulting increased susceptibility to infectious disease), and general inattention to matters of health can be ascribed to preoccupation with the need for the drug and indifference to other drives.

Insensitivity to the warning signal of pain makes him neglect conditions such as appendicitis, burns, and minor injuries. Drowsiness increases his proneness to accidents of all sorts. Nonsterile techniques of injection and impurities in the drugs he uses lead to abscesses, hepatitis, and serious infections. The use of hypodermic needles in common with other addicts may spread diseases such as malaria and syphilis. Frequent intravenous injections cause thrombophlebitis, making veins unavailable for emergency administration of blood or plasma. Lastly, the addict may unknowingly take a lethal dose ("overdose") of an opiate, since the concentration of the drug he purchases is unstandardized and highly variable.

Drug addiction is also not associated with increased incidence of psychosis or of an organic variety of intellectual deterioration. Only 55 out of 125,000 admissions to state mental hospitals in New York between 1946 and 1951 were attributed to the use of opiates (Committee on Public Health Relations of the New York Academy of Medicine, p. 25). Recently, however, a higher incidence of psychosis, particularly depressive reactions, has been seen among middle-class addicts, probably on the basis of failing to realize their social-class vocational aspirations despite failure genuinely to internalize them. The lower class and blacks and Puerto Ricans more frequently develop schizophrenic reactions,* since, having internalized no middle-class vocational aspirations whatsoever, they do not experience a sense of defeat in failing to realize them and simply withdraw from adult reality and responsibility.

Woody and his associates (1975) have suggested that the decrease in catecholamines† associated with withdrawal of narcotics contributes to depression in some addicts undergoing spontaneous or medically regulated detoxification. In any case, detoxification is obviously contra-indicated in addicts suffering from depressive reactions, both for this reason and because it increases self-critical tendencies on psychopharmacological grounds.

---

* Clinical evidence from my own Harlem (lower-class) patients (Ausubel, Karsten, and Ausubel, 1978).

† Catecheholamines are neuro-transmittor brain ammines that facilitate or transmit the passage of the neural impulse at certain central synaptic junctions.

Chapter 3
Psychological Characteristics of Opiate Addiction

Selective Incidence

Thus far, in trying to account for the cause of opiate addiction, we have reached the following conclusions:

(1) Opiates are addicting chiefly because of their euphoria-producing properties which have adjustive value for certain psychologically predisposed persons;

(2) After addiction to an opiate drug is firmly established, a number of relatively permanent changes occur in the addict's personality structure (for example, in the relative strength of various drives, in habitual ways of adjusting to stress) which further augment whatever preexisting tendencies originally led to his addiction;

(3) In order for addiction to take place, access to the drug is necessary.

Still unanswered, however, are questions such as these: Why are the euphoria-producing properties of opiates adjustive for some persons but not for others? Why do not all persons exposed to narcotic drugs avail themselves of the euphoria they can obtain from their use? If some individuals are more susceptible to narcotic addiction than others, which personality traits contribute most to this predisposition?

27

Satisfactory answers to these questions must await the collection of more systematic and exhaustive research data on the personality development of drug addicts (as compared to nonaddicts) than are currently available. Lacking such definitive evidence, we can only utilize the extensive preaddiction developmental data we do have (supplemented by clinical and experimental findings on the behavioral effects of opiates, and by logical inferences regarding the types of personality defects for which euphoria would be adjustive) to construct a plausible theory of the personality factors that make for addiction proneness. But before we turn to this task, let us first examine some theories that have tried to explain the selective occurrence of drug addiction *without* assuming the existence of any predisposing personality traits.

The theory of differential availability of opiates explains in part why most predisposed persons never become addicted (i.e., they are never in contact with drugs). What it fails to explain is why only a small minority of exposed individuals (for example, physicians, pharmacists, slum-dwellers) *do* become addicted. To account for this selective incidence of narcotism among comparably exposed persons, sociologists have suggested the existence of differential degrees of attitudinal tolerance toward addiction on the part of the potential addict's immediate and wider social milieu. As we shall see later, this theory is very helpful in explaining why addiction is more prevalent in one of two equally exposed cultures and why the incidence of addiction can vary widely for different neighborhoods within a highly exposed slum area. Nevertheless, predisposing personality factors are still necessary to account for the selective occurrence of addiction among certain individuals within a small homogeneous group in which both exposure and group tolerance are relatively uniform for all group members. Not all individuals in a highly tolerant social milieu become addicted, and not infrequently some individuals in a highly intolerant social milieu do acquire the drug habit.

In other words, in addition to the actual physical availability of the drug, the likelihood of addiction is also affected by the attitudes of the various social groups with whom the exposed individual identifies. This factor, however, supplements rather than negates or replaces the factor of individual susceptibility.

A much less credible theory has been proposed by Lindesmith (1947), who postulates that an individual becomes addicted when he realizes that opiates can relieve symptoms of distress which he perceives to be caused by the withdrawal of drugs. This merely reiterates the psychological basis of habit formation. It states that adjustive habits become established and reinforced when their causal relationship to certain satisfactions is understood.

Hence, it is clear:

(1) that unless an individual experiences pleasure or relief of distress from the use of opiates and attributes these sensations to such use he is unlikely to become addicted, and

(2) that *realization* of physical or psychological dependence on drugs is probably an essential precondition for the establishment of addiction. It is also understandable that motivations acquired during the course of habituation to drugs help to maintain and to perpetuate addiction.

It is equally clear, however, that the statement that addicts use and continue to use drugs because they find them satisfying neither explains the reason for the satisfaction nor the selective incidence of addiction. Why, in the first place, do only a small minority of persons with access to drugs start using them habitually? Why do certain persons find drugs more pleasurable than others and continue to avail themselves of such pleasure permanently for adjustive purposes?

Lindesmith's (1947) reliance on the discredited proposition that physiological dependence is of crucial importance in addiction and his denial that addicts experience euphoria create additional difficulties. To explain the fact that most persons who develop physiological dependence after receiving opiates for therapeutic purposes do not become addicted, he speculates that some individuals are differentially sensitive to withdrawal symptoms.* However, as long as the differential sensitivity is not explained, this explanation merely begs the question, for on what basis are some persons more sensitive than

---

* Dole and Nyswander (1967) like Lindesmith, consider drug addiction a metabolic disorder; but postulate that prolonged use of heroin causes relatively permanent intracellular changes giving rise to a "tissue craving" for heroin. They similarly discount the influence of personality predispositions. The credibility of this theory is discussed in relation to methadone maintenance therapy (p. 97).

others? Furthermore, the fact that all addicts appreciate the connection between injection of opiates and relief of withdrawal symptoms does not prove that this is the only or central causal factor in addiction. The physiological dependence theory still cannot adequately account for the terrible social price addicts are willing to pay for their addiction, the frequency of relapse, the tendency for addicts to increase their dosage and to use the intravenous route, and for the addictiveness of opiatelike drugs such as methadone, in which abstinence symptoms are relatively mild.

Lindesmith's point is well taken that more preaddiction developmental data (as well as control data on nonaddict populations) are necessary to establish definitively the contribution of personality predispositions to the causation of drug addiction. By the same token, however, the very same kind of data is required to demonstrate that personality predispositions play no role whatsoever in the drug addiction process. The situational approach of Lindesmith (1947) and Becker (1953), which relies exclusively on interview data relating to the current onset and course of addiction, has even less empirical basis on which to formulate a judgment regarding the relative importance of developmental personality factors in vulnerability to addiction.

Wikler (1953, 1977) proposes a conditioning theory of addiction which is essentially not too different from that of Lindesmith (1947) or of Dole and Nyswander (1967). Although he too discounts the importance of personality predispositions, he relies completely on conditioning to explain both the original addiction and subsequent readdictions. Unlike Lindesmith, he doesn't fall back on selective sensitivity to the withdrawal syndrome, or on altered intracellular metabolism giving rise to tissue hunger or "craving" (Dole and Nyswander). As already pointed out, this theory cannot explain the selective incidence of chronic narcotism in only a small percentage of youth and young adults living in an urban ghetto area where both attitudinal tolerance toward the drug and the availability of the drug are high.

Lastly, brief mention may be made of the addict's own explanation of his addiction. By far the most common explanation he offers is association with other addicts coupled with abnormal curiosity. Other favorite explanations include relief from alcoholic hangovers, amelioration of pain, and carelessness on the part of the physician. Female and physician addicts more frequently offer medical explanations. After physical dependence sets in, many addicts claim they perpetuate the habit "just to keep normal."

Although these explanations are of incidental interest in indicating how addicts become introduced to drugs, they obviously have no real bearing on the selective incidence of addiction. Our problem at this point is not to ascertain the channels through which addicts are first introduced to drugs, but to understand why these particular persons, and not many others who are equally exposed, actually become addicted. The addict's testimony could be more helpful with regard to this latter point if it were more reliable and less colored by rationalizations that invariably place the blame on others or on conditions beyond his control.

More Permanent Psychological Effects

The fact that single doses of opiates produce euphoria in addicts is relatively unimportant. In and of itself it constitutes no evidence of any lasting psychological change attributable to drug addiction. The real danger in addiction lies in the more permanent change it induces in characteristic drive-motivated, drive-satisfying, and adjustive behavior. Drug addiction first becomes harmful when it gives rise to a changed way of life, that is, when the desire for euphoria permanently replaces all other socially useful drives, when activity satisfying the need for drugs replaces all other drive-satisfying activities, and when drug use becomes the primary adjustive mechanism in an individual's behavior repertory. This possibility of permanent change in the personality structure of drug addicts is naturally dependent upon two factors: the euphoria-producing properties of opiates, and a predisposing personality makeup for which drug-induced euphoria is both adjustive and satisfying as an end in itself.

The clinical histories of drug addicts are replete with evidence that, once addicted, the majority of these individuals lose interest in productive labor, food, sex, companionship, family ties, and recreation (Pescor, 1938; Wikler, 1944). They become undependable, neglectful of other responsibilities, lethargic, and slovenly. These impressions have been substantiated by controlled observations of experimentally addicted postaddicts which show that

> the addict's sphere of interests becomes more and more constricted until most of the time he is preoccupied with "enjoying" the effects of the last injection and getting ready for the next. Assigned duties may be discharged satisfactorily [only] if such performance is necessary to insure good relations with the sources of the drug supply (Wikler, 1953).

Other studies of experimental addiction demonstrate that morphine makes an addict more suggestible and less responsive to situational threat. The latter effect is partially achieved by blunting sensitivity to such environmental threats as pain and hunger which ordinarily provoke marked adjustive responses in most persons. We shall return to these data again in discussing why opiates are especially adjustive to individuals with certain personality defects.

The demonstrably poorer social adjustment achieved by addicts subsequent to addiction is attributable both to the replacement of normal drives by the need for opiates and to the socially unacceptable status of drug addiction. The typical addict must devote considerable time to procuring his supply of drugs, and, what is worse, their high price usually drives him to criminal activity. He therefore finds it almost impossible to hold down a steady job and engage in socially useful activity—even if he has the inclination. Hence, he not only leads a useless and economically wasteful life, but also preys on the resources of family, friends, and society in general. Almost invariably (except in the case of physician and wealthy addicts), addiction leads to a marginal economic existence. In his desperate and clandestine struggle to gratify his craving for drugs, whatever tendencies toward deceit, dishonesty, and unreliability already exist are inevitably reinforced.

Drug addiction also has an adverse influence on marital adjustment and interpersonal relationships. One-third of a typical population of adult male drug addicts was unmarried, and another third reported marital dissension and broken marriages over the use of drugs (Pescor, 1938). Clinical interviews and psychological tests show that addiction leads to more seclusive, asocial, and introverted behavior. Adolescent addicts tend to become truant, to withdraw from the social group, and to break relations with their girl friends (Zimmering, 1952).

In general, drug addiction does not significantly impair intelligence or psychological efficiency. Drug addicts are able to work skillfully and efficiently if they want to, although speed may be reduced. Studies show a loss of speed in motor tasks, in verbal and motor reaction time, in verbal learning (Isbell, 1951), and in computational work. It is highly doubtful, however, "if this degree of impairment is of significant practical importance" (Wikler, 1953). Much more important than any loss in performance ability is the addict's loss of interest in and disinclination for work unrelated to the procurement of his drug supply.

A universally observed phenomenon in addiction treatment centers is the rarity of addicts 50 years of age and over. This is attributable to a process of delayed personality maturation among them in their late thirties and early forties (Winick, 1963). They seem spontaneously to "burn out" and renounce addicting drugs—to settle down to a more conventional vocational and family existence. This is especially true in wartime when, as observed later, illicit drugs are practically unobtainable and addicts are able to find well-paying jobs in war-production industries (due to an increased need for manpower and a consequent lessening of job discrimination against them). It is as if the adult personality maturation that ordinarily occurs in nonaddicts during late childhood and adolescence takes 30 years longer in addiction-prone inadequate personalities. It is also an indictment of society's extra-legal punitive and discriminatory attitudes toward ex-addicts (despite fair employment laws) which greatly militates against their rehabilitation by making normal vocational adjustment extremely difficult and making relapse to drug abuse accordingly more attractive. Periods of economic depression have the same effects because addicts holding jobs in good times tend to be the first to be fired as unemployment rises.

Multiple Causality in Disease

Generally speaking, research on drug addiction has been hampered by the same type of faulty thinking that has plagued the investigation of the causes of such other complex disorders as cancer, tuberculosis, and juvenile delinquency. This is the error of assuming that since the disorder in question *appears* to be identical in all individuals, it must necessarily have the same *single* cause in all instances. Actually, there are many different kinds of drug addicts, and the causes of drug addiction are multiple and additive in their impact rather than mutually exclusive.

As in most other diseases, the causes of drug addiction include both *internal* factors originating within the affected individual (e.g., hereditary susceptibility) and *external* factors originating within the environment. Each type of factor may be further categorized with respect to whether its impact occurs immediately prior to, and is essential for, the appearance of the disease (*precipitating*), or operates over a longer period of time and is largely contributory (*predisposing*).

In tuberculosis, for example, hereditary susceptibility to the inroads of tubercle bacilli is the predisposing internal cause, and temporary lowering of general resistance (as in overexertion or exposure to extremes of temperature) is the precipitating internal cause. Comparable external causes would include overcrowded living conditions, on the one hand, and actual exposure to an adequately large dose of virulent tubercle bacilli, on the other.

It makes little sense, therefore, to talk about *the* cause of tuberculosis. Exposure to a reasonably large dose of virulent organisms is a necessary causal factor but is rarely a sufficient cause in the absence of particular hereditary susceptibility to tuberculosis, depressed standards of living, and transitory lapses in general resistance to disease. In any given case, one particular factor may overshadow all others and thus provide a spurious appearance of single causality; but this neither guarantees that this same factor will be equally prominent in other cases nor excludes the operation of other factors in the same case. All we can say in this regard, is that if any one of the relevant causes is especially salient, the other contributory factors are less necessary to bring about the disease.

If one individual, for example, by virtue of his heredity, happened to be highly susceptible to tuberculosis, whereas his neighbor happened to be highly resistant to this disease, the former would obviously succumb to a much smaller dose of tubercle bacilli than would be necessary to strike down the latter. It also follows that both the severity of the disease and the outlook for recovery would vary in accordance with the relative prominence of the various causal factors.

Multiple Causality in Drug Addiction

The causal picture in drug addiction is quite analogous to that just described for tuberculosis. Availability of narcotics (that is, exposure to addicts and drug peddlers, or, in the case of physicians and others, even more direct access to the drug) is the external precipitating factor. No matter how great an individual's susceptibility on personality grounds, he obviously cannot become a drug addict unless he has regular access to narcotics. The factor of relative availability explains why the rate of addiction is so much higher in slum areas and among members of the medical and allied professions than in middle-class neighborhoods and among other occupational groups. To account for the higher Puerto Rican addiction rate in comparably exposed black and Puerto Rican sections of New York City's Harlem slum area (Committee on Public Health Relations, New York Academy of Medicine, 1953, p. 64), and for the much higher addiction rate in China than in Japan (Merrill, 1942), one must invoke a major predisposing factor, also of environmental origin, namely, degree of community or cultural tolerance for the practice.

But *external* factors alone cannot explain all of the known facts about the incidence and distribution of drug addiction. In a given slum area of uniformly high exposure to and tolerance for the drug addiction habit, why is the practice limited to a relatively small minority of the residents, and why do male adolescents constitute such a disproportionately large percentage of the affected group? Why do some addicts originate in middle-class neighborhoods despite little exposure to narcotics and strong community disapproval of the habit? To explain these facts, we must turn to the important *internal* factor of differential susceptibility. In the same sense that individuals are not equally susceptible to tuberculosis, they are not equally susceptible to drug addiction.

Classification

We have seen that various theorists have been unsuccessful in explaining convincingly the selective incidence of drug addiction as long as they have denied the operation of predisposing personality factors. Our next task, therefore, is to classify drug addicts on the basis of personality predispositions that determine relative degree of susceptibility to addiction. The most acceptable source of data for constructing such a classification lies in clinical histories of the preaddiction personality development of different types of drug addicts. It should be realized, however, that in the absence of adequate control data, any classification must necessarily be tentative in nature.*

The most defensible classification in the light of available evidence distinguishes between three basic categories of opiate addiction (Ausubel, 1948):

(1) *primary* addiction, in which opiates have specific adjustive value for particular personality defects;

(2) *symptomatic* addiction, in which the use of opiates has no particular adjustive value and is only an incidental symptom of behavior disorder; and

(3) *reactive* addiction, in which drug use is a transitory developmental phenomenon in essentially normal individuals influenced by distorted peer-group norms alienated from adult society.

In a larger sense, all three major varieties of addiction have adjustive functions. The difference between primary and symptomatic addiction is mainly a difference in the specificity of the adjustive value of opiate-induced euphoria for the personality disturbance involved. Reactive addiction, on the other hand, is adjustive for developmental and situational stress or for conformity needs in a peer group and not for a serious personality defect.

Apart from its value in clarifying the nature of the drug addiction process, the practical importance of distinguishing among these

---

* Further support for this classification comes from (a) the introspective reports of addicts in describing the psychological effects of opiates during the course of clinical or experimental addiction, (b) psychological experiments dealing with the influence of opiates on behavior in stressful situations, (c) observations of institutional behavior of addicts, and (d) logical inferences regarding the probable adjustive value of opiates for different kinds of personality disorders.

three categories of addicts will become especially apparent in our discussion of treatment and prognosis. Also, from an educational standpoint, it is extremely important to counteract the widespread misconceptions that everybody is susceptible and equally susceptible to addiction and that all addicts are suffering from the same kind of disease. Parents and teachers will be relieved to learn that "only individuals with . . . very special kinds of personality defects can become truly addicted to drugs, and that only a very small proportion of new adolescent [narcotic users] become permanent addicts" (Ausubel, 1952a).

This classification is thought to be superior to the widely used Kolb (1925) classification, which is purely descriptive in nature and which makes no attempt to distinguish among addicts on the basis of the adjustive benefit they receive from opiates. Three of the six categories used by Kolb are extremely difficult to justify in practice. Psychotic reactions due to opiate use are rare, relatively idiosyncratic, and seldom chronic. Normal individuals accidentally addicted are also rare and are not true addicts since their addiction is based chiefly on physical dependence and has little adjustive value in a psychological sense. The "inebriate personality" merely identifies a group of addicts who have nothing in common except a prior history of alcoholism. Kolb's neurotic group really consists of individuals with mild anxiety states and reactive depressions. They are not serious neurotics and constitute an atypical variety of primary addiction. His "psychopathic diathesis" is a vague term for the basic personality defect ("inadequate personality") associated with primary drug addiction. Lastly, his psychopathic personality characterizes the antisocial psychopath for whom addiction is only one minor symptomatic outlet for the expression of hostility and aggression.

Primary Addiction

Primary drug addiction includes all addicts with personality trends for which addiction to drugs has *specific* adjustive value. Two subgroups may be delineated: (a) the inadequate personality, and (b) anxiety and reactive depression states. Of these two subgroups, the inadequate personality constitutes the numerically more important and prognostically less-hopeful variety. Since drug addiction is an almost tailor-made adjustive mechanism for this psychological disorder, it may be regarded as the characteristic personality makeup predisposing individuals to opiate addiction. For the other personality trends, the adjustive value of addiction is less specific and less efficient; hence, incidence is lower, prognosis better, and the consequences to both society and the individual less disastrous.

The Inadequate Personality

The basic characteristic of the inadequate personality is a defect which we can call motivational immaturity.

> This is a condition in which the goals of an individual and his methods of achieving goals fail to undergo normal maturation [during preadolescence and adolescence]. Hence, as an adult he displays the motivational maturity of a child.
>   By the time an individual reaches late adolescence in our culture we can normally expect certain evidences of goal maturation to take place. We can expect him to aspire to a status that he attains through his own efforts rather than to one that he [acquires] merely by virtue of a dependent relationship to his parents. We can expect him to formulate his own goals and reach decisions independently; to be less dependent on parental approval; to be able to postpone immediate pleasure-seeking goals for the sake of advancing long-range objectives; and to continue striving despite initial setbacks. We can expect him to aspire to realistic goals; to be capable of judging himself, his accomplishments, and his prospects with a certain amount of critical ability; and to have acquired a sense of moral obligation and responsibility (Ausubel, 1952a).

The inadequate personality fails to conceive of himself as an independent adult and fails to identify with such normal adult goals as financial independence, stable employment, and the establishment of his own home and family. He is passive, dependent, unreliable, and unwilling to postpone immediate gratification of pleasurable impulses. He demonstrates no desire to persevere in the face of environmental difficulties, or to accept responsibilities which he finds distasteful. His preoccupation with a search for effortless pleasure represents both an inappropriate persistence of childhood motivations, which he has not as yet outgrown, and a regressive form of compensation for his inability to obtain satisfaction from adult goals.

But although he is, by any criterion, a highly inadequate and immature person he does not have sufficient self-critical ability to perceive himself as such. In fact, this blunting of his self-critical faculty is partly a defensive device which enables him to preserve a serene self-portrait and appraisal of his present circumstances and future prospects in the face of conditions that would produce overwhelming feelings of inadequacy in others. It also spares him the effort, the planning, and the self-discipline that would be required for effecting sincere improvement.

Clinical Evidence

Although clinical evidence is relatively scanty, it generally substantiates the view that the majority of drug addicts conform to this description of the inadequate personality. Psychiatric history and examination and a battery of psychological tests reveal the following picture of adolescent heroin addicts treated at Bellevue Hospital: motivational inertia, lack of motivation at work and in school, low frustration and anxiety tolerance, inability to concentrate effort, constriction of interests; passive, dependent, and narcissistic personality trends; abnormally strong attachment to mother; superficial and easily disrupted interpersonal relationships; superficial social maturity; tendency toward withdrawal, regressive, and fantasy adjustive techniques (Ausubel, 1947; Zimmering, 1951, 1952a).

Representative clinical studies of adult drug addicts yield essentially the same results. Fifty-five percent of 1,036 drug addicts at the U.S. Public Health Service Hospital were classified as manifesting "psychopathic diathesis," a diagnostic category roughly equivalent to inadequate personality (Pescor, 1939). These individuals exhibited a marginal economic adjustment (nomadism, irregular employment, frequent change of employment) prior to addiction, unsatisfactory social adjustment subsequent to addiction, and an unstable marital history. They were tolerant to all forms of thrill-seeking vice, to alcoholism, and to addiction to other drugs (Ausubel, 1947). Fifty-eight percent of 318 adult addicts at Bellevue Hospital were diagnosed as inadequate, emotionally unstable, or nomadic personalities. Psychiatric and psychological examination of 37 women addicts at the state Reformatory for Women in Illinois resulted in a diagnosis of inadequate personality in 21 cases. And after prolonged interviews with 40 addicts in the Chicago area, Bingham Dai (1937) concluded that an inadequate, infantile, and emotionally unstable personality characterized by undue dependence on others and social irresponsibility was the essential predisposing factor in drug addiction.

A prior history of drug addiction in naval recruits is associated with less effective military performance and more evidence of emotional pathology in all adjustment areas than is the case with recruits who have no prior history of drug use (Plag et al., 1975).

The early childhood history of this variety of drug addict is apparently quite normal. There is no evidence of undue rejection by parents, of discordant family relationships, or of broken homes. In comparison with a group of delinquent adolescents, however, the Bellevue group of adolescent drug addicts seemed excessively attached to their mothers. Without pointing to the precise source or nature of the difficulty, Dai's data led him to conclude that the genesis of the characteristic infantile personality he observed among drug addicts was to be found in a disturbed parent-child relationship. But by analogy to the developmental history typical of most inadequate personalities, we can infer that the maturational defect is not attributable to lack of emotional acceptance by parents during the preschool years. It develops instead during the later period when there is normally a transference of emotional identification from childhood goals and goal-seeking patterns to their adult counterparts.

Three kinds of child-rearing patterns during middle childhood and preadolescence are especially detrimental to the development of motivational immaturity. They are typified by

> (1) the extremely *overprotecting* parent who shields the child from all independent experience and all possibility of failure so that he never gets the opportunity to set mature goals for himself or to act independently; (2) the extremely *overpermissive* parent, who makes no demands on the child for mature behavior and leads him to believe that he is a specially privileged person whose needs will always be satisfied by others; and (3) the extremely *overdominating* parent who imposes excessively high goals on the child, thereby inviting complete sabotage of the goals of adult maturation as soon as he can escape from parental control (Ausubel, 1952a).

These three types of child-rearing patterns were in fact found significantly more frequently than in a group of matched controls in the Public Health Service Hospital at Lexington (Ausubel, 1947). Merry (1972) found a more unstable home environment among addicts than in a nonaddict control population.

Adjustive Value of Drug Addiction

The inadequate personality who fails to identify with mature adult goals is primarily concerned with achieving two adjustive objectives: (1) the creation of a hedonistically structured environment for himself in which he can pursue effortless, pleasure-seeking activities; and (2) the shutting out of the intrusive demands and responsibilities associated with adult personality status. As an essentially extroverted individual who relishes direct emotional participation in experience, he prefers (unlike the schizophrenic) to structure his hedonistic psychological world within a semirealistic and not a fantasy framework.

Drug addiction is ideally suited for realizing these adjustive objectives. After he takes his first few shots the addict literally exclaims, "Boy, this is what I've been looking for all of my life. What could be easier?" By merely injecting a needle under his skin he satisfies his quest for immediate and effortless pleasure. Apart from the voluptuous thrill of the "kick," he reports increased self-confidence and feelings of self-esteem, decreased anxiety, and grandiose fantasies of wealth, power, and omnipotence. Primary needs such as hunger and sex urges fade into the background, and, although not directly gratified, are rendered so uninsistent as to be incapable of generating anxiety or frustration when their satisfaction is threatened or denied. Fear of pain is also set aside as the threshold for pain perception is raised and as its anxiety-producing implications are minimized.

In fact, because of the drug's specific inhibition of the self-critical faculty, the environment in general assumes a generally more benevolent and less-threatening aspect. With the help of opiates,

> the addict becomes easily contented with his inadequate, hedonistic adjustment to life and is more easily able to evade and overlook responsibilities. . . . In the absence of any actual accomplishment he feels supremely satisfied with himself and his future. By virtue of

its . . . general dulling effect on consciousness, the drug provides a
partial escape from the disturbing and distasteful elements of reality.
Thus if he is actually required to work and assume responsibility, the
hard distasteful edge of the task is softened, much in the way a self-
indulged child will fulfill his chores as long as he has a lollipop in his
mouth (Ausubel, 1948).

Once established, drug addiction is reinforced by "memory
associations and habits that are built up by the practice over long
periods of time of relieving mental and physical distress and pain"
and of procuring instantaneous satisfaction merely by inserting a
needle under the skin. It becomes a highly preemptive adjustive
technique, its applicability generalizing to distress of any origin.
Because of its tremendous efficiency, it displaces other adjustive
mechanisms and soon becomes the sole adequate source of need-
satisfaction. Also, as physiological dependence is developed, a new
primarylike need is established which only opiates can satisfy. This
ever-present possibility of experiencing dramatic relief from the
drug enhances its euphoria-producing powers, and addicts deliber-
ately postpone injection of the drug until mild abstinence symptoms
occur.

Experimental Evidence

Additional insight into the adjustive properties of opiates comes
from studies of their effects on experimental neuroses in animals and
on conflict-produced disruption of performance in human subjects.
In both instances, morphine abolishes unadaptive, phobic, compulsive, and anxiety-ridden responses (Masserman, 1946). One obvious
way in which it does this is by reducing motivational conflict. If
either pain or hunger constitutes one of a pair of mutually
antagonistic motivational stimuli, or if anticipation or avoidance of
pain is part of a conflictful situation, elimination of these primary
drives (pain or hunger) self-evidently resolves the conflict and the
unadaptive behavior it engenders. Responsiveness to situational
threat is reduced when the individual no longer needs or desires
what the environment threatens to deprive him of, or when he is
indifferent to the punishment or frustration implicit in unsuccessful
adaptation.

Morphine also abolishes unadaptive behavior (induced by experimental stress situations) by reinstating the habitual behavior of the

organism that prevailed prior to the stress experience (Masserman, 1946; Wikler and Masserman, 1943). This reinstatement, however, will obviously be an improvement only if the habitual prestress behavior is more normal than the new unadaptive neurotic behavior induced by stress. If, for example, we start out with chronically neurotic cats and induce a different kind of neurotic behavior by means of experimental stress, morphine will abolish the new neurotic behavior and reinstate the old chronic neurotic behavior. This is no improvement. However, if the cat (or human) were normal to begin with, morphine would reinstate habitual normal behavior.

Thus, morphine has adjustive value for the inadequate personality because it reduces his responsiveness to situational threat, releases more adaptive behavior, and reinstates his casual, indifferent, and irresponsible orientation to life whenever it threatens to be inundated by insistently disturbing elements in the current psychological field. In the case of a motivationally mature individual, on the other hand, morphine similarly reduces situational threat and releases more normal and habitual adaptive behavior; but, at the same time, it reinforces his mature adult strivings, his sense of responsibility and his normal goal-directed activities. Hence, opiate addiction can never constitute a complete and an adequate substitute for the satisfaction of genuine drives in a motivationally mature person. It can at best alleviate situationally induced anxiety or depression in normal individuals or their situationally aggravated counterparts in anxiety-prone individuals.

Anxiety States and Reactive Depression

A relatively rare form of primary addiction is found in states of anxiety and reactive depression. Six percent of the patients at the Lexington, Kentucky, hospital are classified as psychoneurotic (Pescor, 1938). In private hospitals and in private practice (Rado, 1933), the incidence is higher because such addicts, who use heroin to cope with symptoms of anxiety and depression (Khantzian et al., 1974), are better able to maintain a satisfactory economic adjustment.

However, in a representative population of addicts (for example, the Lexington group), neither anxiety nor depression is a prominent symptom, and rarely is either striking enough to warrant a diagnosis of psychoneurosis (Ausubel, 1947; Pescor, 1938). The electroencephalograms of most addicts during withdrawal also fail to show any more evidence of anxiety than during active addiction (Andrews, 1941), as one might reasonably anticipate if the purpose of using and the effect of the drug were to reduce excessive anxiety.

The reasons for the limited adjustive value of opiates for anxiety and depression* inhere in the personality structure of persons with these disorders. The latter individuals, far from being motivationally immature, are characterized by extremely high aspirations for success and by very persistent strivings. In part, these high ambitions are meant to compensate for a lack of intrinsic self-esteem, a product of unsatisfactory parent-child relationships resulting from either parental rejection or acceptance for extrinsic considerations (vicarious ego satisfactions from the child's achievements). Because impaired self-esteem makes them feel inadequate to cope with their environment, they tend to overreact with fear to environmental situations that pose a further threat to self-esteem—feelings of inadequacy and depression, and disruption of adaptive behavior. In addition, self-esteem is constantly threatened by the improbability of attaining the unrealistically high goals which they set for themselves.

In contrast to addicts with the diagnosis of inadequate personality, psychoneurotic addicts, as children, are considered studious, shut-in, "good-boy" types. They tend to have a college education, a professional or semiprofessional type of occupation, a good marital adjustment, and an acceptable economic adjustment despite addiction. They give a history of military service, of several voluntary attempts at cure, and of relapses to drug addiction because of environmental stress and worry. In the institution, they are socially unpopular with their fellow patients (Pescor, 1938).

The attractiveness of opiates for these individuals lies in their ability to reduce emotional responsiveness to situational threat and to disintegrate stress-induced maladaptive behavior. Stress is made more tolerable and the environment seems less foreboding. But because of the presence of mature, highly developed, and insistent

---

* Minnesota Multiphasic Inventory (MMPI) profiles of addicts exhibit elevations on the manic, depressive, and psychopathic deviate sides (Hill, Haertzen, and Davis, 1962).

adult goals, the ephemeral hedonistic satisfactions that opiates can offer are insufficient as ends in themselves. The drug is valued for its sedative, anxiety-reducing properties, and for its ability to soften the unreasonably harsh and critical view that anxious or depressed individuals take of themselves. Since the latter addicts are less interested in the pleasurable effects of opiates, they are more able to limit themselves to smaller, stabilized doses. And since the drug serves to reinforce basic personality trends and reaction tendencies, mature, socially productive, and responsible vocational, and interpersonal activities are not seriously interfered with.

The relative rarity of this variety of drug addiction, therefore, can be ascribed in part to the less specific, complete, and efficient adjustive value of opiates for the personality structure underlying chronic anxiety states and recurrent depressions. In addition, many other adjustive techniques of comparable value (for example, rationalization, projection, compulsiveness) are available. Such persons also are extremely sensitive to the loss of social status that stigmatization as a drug addict would bring. Hence, unless the drug is both extremely accessible and obtainable with little risk of apprehension (as in the medical and allied professions), addiction is very unlikely to be chosen as the preferred adjustive technique.

Symptomatic Addiction

Symptomatic drug addiction occurs primarily as a nonspecific symptom in aggressive antisocial personalities.* The main disorder itself is a form of gross moral agenesis in which the individual fails to internalize any obligations whatsoever to conform to the ethical standards of society. He is a remorseless, predatory, and incorrigible delinquent full of contempt for others and driven by hostile, aggressive impulses and deep-seated resentments. Of the various types of deviant drug addicts, he alone finds incentive in the illegality of addiction.

Drug addiction has no *particular* adjustive value for this type of person. It is only one minor symptomatic outlet (chosen if available) for the expression of his antisocial and aggressive trends.

---

* In the current *Diagnostic Nomenclature II* of the American Psychiatric Association, such individuals are classified as *sociopaths*. In the writer's opinion, however, this disorder is less of a personality or character disorder than a serious aberration in the development of conscience.

> The aggressive psychopath feels that through drug addiction he is getting one more unearned, socially disapproved, and forbidden extra thrill out of life and is thereby "getting even" with society (Ausubel, 1948).

He presents a history of delinquency from early childhood, and invariably has a preaddiction antisocial record. Addiction is a relatively inconspicuous incident in the delinquent careers of antisocial psychopaths. The crimes they commit are not precipitated by the drugs they take. In fact, since opiates actually inhibit aggressive impulses, they make psychopaths less likely to commit crimes of violence. Unfortunately, however, these atypical addicts, who constitute only a very small minority of the total addict population, lend credence to the popular misconception that narcotic addiction leads to violent crime and that drug addicts are fiendish, cold-blooded criminals.

Reactive Addiction

Reactive drug addiction is essentially an adolescent phenomenon. It has no adjustive value for any basic personality defect. It is a response to transitory developmental pressures, a vehicle for the expression of antiadult sentiments, and a means of obtaining acceptance in certain slum-urban peer groups.

Naturally, all adolescent drug addicts cannot be placed in the category of reactive addiction. Many, perhaps 15 to 20 percent, are simply inadequate personalities, reactive depressives, anxiety neurotics, or psychopathic deviates whose addiction careers begin in adolescence. However, the vast majority of recent adolescent addicts are essentially normal boys and girls who have merely temporarily dabbled in, or provisionally experimented with, drugs in the course of growing up in an exposed urban environment. This type of experimentation is very similar to the transitory delinquency, alcoholism, and homosexuality which are very common in adolescence but which, by and large, do not terminate in adult criminality, addiction to alcohol or sexual inversion.

But even though reactive and adolescent drug addiction are not synonymous, all adolescent drug addicts do have certain characteristics in common.

In the first place, they have less money than adults and can less afford the regular and high dosage of adulterated opiates necessary to produce physiological dependence. Thus, there are incomparably more drug users than drug addicts. Only the intrinsically more serious cases become physically dependent. The others are more apt to indulge in occasional "joy-pops."

Second, since they have not as yet had time to learn a trade or vocation, they are more completely dependent upon crime and prostitution to support their habits. For the same reason, and also because they wish to rationalize their habits and retain their acceptance in the peer group, they are more likely to engage in a proselytizing form of drug peddling.

Third, the sequence of initiation to drug use is typical, beginning with marihuana, and proceeding to sniffing and subcutaneous and intravenous injection of heroin.

Last, the onset of addiction in adolescents is associated with truancy, withdrawal from the gang, congregation in smaller social units, and rupture of relationships with girl friends.

Behavioral Significance

Reactive addiction is largely a nonspecific aggressive response to the prolonged status deprivation to which adolescents are subjected in our society. Like truancy, delinquency, and the hippie culture, it is expressive of a general antiadult orientation characterized by defiance of traditional norms and conventions and flouting of adult-imposed taboos and authority. For some adolescents, it has the same fascination as other exaggerated prerogatives of adult status, such as premature use of alcohol and tobacco and reckless automobile driving. It appeals to their bravado, their curiosity about forbidden pleasures, their need for excitement and adventure, and their inclination to experiment with danger, mystery, and romance. These motives are especially characteristic of adolescents who are overactive, impulsive, and headstrong, but not necessarily psychopathic in their moral outlook. Under other circumstances, similar traits are associated with transitory delinquency.

During the postwar era, such thrill-seeking attitudes became increasingly generalized among the adolescent populations of many nations, and, in a very real sense, have contributed to the worldwide "epidemic" of juvenile addiction. They reflect

> a more recent condition of permanent international crisis and insecurity that seems to be making a mockery of planning and striving on an individual basis. This gives rise to a philosophy of existentialism, to a feeling that one might just as well try everything that human beings can experience before the atom bombs start falling (Ausubel, 1952a).

Like other forms of adolescent rebellion, reactive addiction is generated and propagated through peer groups. The individual rebel is impotent and lacks status. He needs the support, the approval, and the encouragement of his peers to persist in his defiance of adult standards. When he has these, his activities become remarkably resistive to influence from other sources. After the key prestige figures in a peer group are converted to transitory drug use, they are able to use the power of group approval and acceptance to coerce the conformity of reluctant individuals. So great is the adolescent's need for status and belongingness in the group that he is willing to sacrifice his individual preferences and convictions for group acceptance. And once addicted, loyalty to the group is even more essential to protect his supply of drugs and to avoid arrest.

For the most part, reactive addiction is a phenomenon of urban slum life (although it is becoming increasingly more common in the suburbs and among middle-class groups). The main reasons for this situation are the greater availability of drugs in slum areas and the greater community tolerance toward drug use in certain of these areas. The illicit traffic in drugs is a characteristic feature of underworld activity in the slums. Just as many boys in these areas normally sample delinquency at one time or another in the course of growing up—because it is part of the cultural pattern—they also sample drugs. Although reactive addiction is an aggressive response to status deprivation, the slum-dwelling individual has other reasons, in addition to membership in the adolescent age group, for manifesting aggressive proclivities. He is also reacting to poverty, overcrowding, circumscription of vocational opportunity, and to racial and ethnic discrimination. He has fewer socially acceptable leisure-time and group activity outlets for his energy and status needs.

To a lesser extent, transitory adolescent drug addiction may also serve two other functions. First, it may be utilized by adolescents who are resistive to, or ambivalent about, undergoing adult maturation. Such phasic trends are exceedingly common during adolescence and, in most instances, do not have a poor prognosis. They can be indulged more successfully under the influence of opiates. Second, opiates have a sedative effect on the particular anxieties and insecurities characteristic of adolescence in the same sense that they do on anxiety of any origin. But unless this anxiety is reflective of basic personality defects, it does not extend beyond the adolescent period.

A final type of transitory, and sometimes chronic, addiction occurs among relatively normal adolescent slum-dwellers (especially blacks, Puerto Ricans, and Mexican-Americans) who feel overwhelmed, hopeless, and desperate about coping with poverty, unemployment, inadequate housing, racial discrimination, and lack of economic opportunity. They seek in narcotics a temporary or permanent escape from the seemingly insoluble problems in their environment. The famous black leader, Malcolm X, was apparently a transitory addict on this basis.

Outcome

Reactive drug addiction is usually a transitory, self-limited phenomenon with no serious or lasting consequences. When the

> rebellious, venturesome, "try anything" adolescent boy who otherwise has a normal personality structure . . . tries drugs, he finds that they have little adjustive value for him because he is really concerned with mature, adult achievement in the real world. To a person with a normal amount of self-critical ability who truly aspires to normal adult status in our culture—i.e., to economic independence, to productive labor, to social acceptance and family life—the benefits that drugs can confer are ephemeral and unsubstantial. Drugs do not help such an individual arrive where he wants to go. Hence, he has his fling and then forgets about the whole business.
>
> By sampling narcotics, he has served his purpose of asserting himself and defying adult authority, just as he would by racing his car at sixty miles an hour through a stop sign, or by coming home dead drunk at three in the morning.

> But he has not made a fatal, irrevocable mistake. . . . He is not caught in the "iron grip" of physiological dependence. . . . This dependence involves a relatively mild and self-limited period of physical suffering when the drug is withdrawn.* And if the drug has no true adjustive value, this is a small price to pay compared to [the exorbitant price] of heroin, ostracism and imprisonment (Ausubel, 1960).

As already pointed out, if would be dangerous and misleading to conclude that all teen-age addicts necessarily belong to the reactive group, and, hence, that adolescent addiction may be blithely dismissed as a benign and transitory fad. Adolescent addicts who manifest the characteristic personality traits found in older addicts diagnosed as inadequate personalities naturally obtain the same adjustive benefits from opiates, and, consequently, present the same basically unfavorable prognosis. In fact, the clinical histories of youthful addicts treated at the Lexington, Bellevue, and Riverside hospitals differ little from those of addicts in general.

However, it should be borne in mind that the teen-age addict who was treated in these hospitals is probably no more representative of the typical adolescent drug user in our urban slum areas than the apprehended juvenile criminal is representative of the typical juvenile delinquent. The youngster whose narcotic or delinquent activities are serious enough to merit the official attention of the police, the school, and the juvenile court is more apt to be an habitual and flagrant offender. For each of these potentially chronic and seriously disturbed cases, there are probably a dozen or more essentially normal boys whose occasional "joy-pops" constitute no more than a phasic symptom of adolescent aggression in a context of severe socioeconomic deprivation.

Such cases are not included in hospital, court, or FBI statistics; however, these impressions are confirmed by normative sociological research (Chein, 1964; Research Center for Human Relations, New York University, 1957). In any event, the seriousness of a given case of adolescent drug addiction can only be ascertained after careful clinical diagnosis. Age per se is valueless as a prognostic indicator.

---

* As previously pointed out, reactive adolescent drug users rarely take sufficient amounts of narcotics regularly enough to become physically dependent on them. More typically, they are recreational weekend "joy-poppers" (i.e., inject the drug hypodermically) or sniffers.

A difficult problem in differential diagnosis is posed by the fact that the motivationally immature type of addict is found most commonly (although by no means as exclusively as is the reactive type of addict) among adolescent and young adult males in urban slum areas. This is hardly surprising, when one considers that motivational immaturity is no more rare in such areas than elsewhere, and that the actual development of addiction in highly susceptible individuals is further abetted by adolescent stresses, gang influences, racial and social class tensions, social demoralization, high availability of narcotics, and high community tolerance for the drug habit. How then does one distinguish between these two basically different types of addicts, both of whom are often represented in the same gang?

Data collected by the Research Center for Human Relations of New York University (1957), Gerard and Kornetsky (1955), and Chein (1964) suggest several feasible criteria for differential diagnosis. Motivationally immature addicts tend to use narcotics more regularly, in larger quantities, and more for their adjustive values than "for kicks." They also tend to manifest more serious and deep-seated personality problems, to be peripheral rather than active members of delinquent gangs, and to participate more in the remunerative, criminal ventures of the gangs than in their athletic, heterosexual, and gang warfare activities. Reactive users, on the othert hand, are typically week-end "joy-poppers" who much more rarely take the drug regularly enough or in sufficient quantity to develop physical dependence. They are more likely to be delinquent before addiction, to come from the economically more-depressed homes in the neighborhood, and to use drugs either to conform to age-mate standards or as just another nonspecific means of expressing antisocial attitudes. After the age of 18, the reactive drug user tends to abandon both his active, predatory gang interests and his casual use of drugs in favor of more mature, conventional concerns with vocation and family; but the motivationally immature habitual user retreats further from normal adult adjustment into drug-induced euphoria.

On the basis of the relative prominence of these various causal factors, it is both possible and diagnostically important to distinguish between these two major and essentially different types of drug abusers. In instances where increased susceptibility to addiction is indicative of long-standing motivational immaturity (the *internal* predisposing factor), the highly specific and efficient adjustive value of the drug makes for a chronic type of disorder with a very poor prognosis. Where *external* causal factors are more prominent and internal factors are of a more temporary (precipitating) nature, the adjustive value of the drug is less specific and efficient, and the resulting (reactive) type of addiction accordingly tends to be a transitory aberration similar to juvenile delinquency. Both types of addiction, however, the motivationally immature as well as the reactive, are found most commonly among adolescent males in the urban slums. This is because motivational immaturity occurs just as or more frequently there as elsewhere, and because all of the other internal and external causal factors (the various developmental and social stresses, the high availability of the drug, the high community tolerance) tend to converge on teen-age boys who reside in such areas.

Use of Other Drugs

To what extent do opiate addicts use other drugs and what is the significance of such use? Many opiate addicts begin their addiction careers as alcoholics or as marihuana users. (Twenty-two percent of the Lexington hospital addicts were classified as inebriate personalities.) Some use cocaine (speedballs) or marihuana simultaneously with their opiates. Since marihuana, cocaine, and the barbiturates will be given separate attention in Chapter 6, this section will be primarily devoted to the relationship between the opiates and alcohol.

That opiate addicts often give a history of prior use of alcohol or marihuana does not necessarily mean that such use is causally related to the incidence of opiate addiction. More parsimonious is the explanation that the same individuals who tend to be exposed to opiates are likely to be exposed first to alcohol and marihuana, since these latter drugs are commonly found in the same social environment and are generally regarded as less extreme forms of addiction.* Furthermore, some experimentation with different kinds of

---

* In fact, although most opiate users have a prior history of marihuana use, the vast majority of marihuana users do not try heroin (Goode, 1970; Robbins et al, 1970).

drugs is necessary before the drug of choice can be finally determined, and there is also considerable overlapping between the effects of the various drugs and between the personality patterns of their typical users.

In support of the concept of specificity of drug preference, however, is the fact that

> although the opiate addict will use other intoxicants when opiate drugs are not available, he will habitually return to the use of the latter in spite of the expense, and the legal and social difficulties which beset him in doing so (Wikler, 1953).

One may reasonably hypothesize that this specificity is related to the particular adjustive value which the effects of opiates have for the personality needs of individuals predisposed to their use. Other drugs simply are not as satisfying or as efficient, and will be used only before experience with opiates is acquired or if the latter drugs are temporarily unavailable. On the other hand, one would anticipate less definite indications of preference in drug users who do not manifest a crystallized personality defect.

The inadequate personality is not satisfied with alcohol because alcohol does not provide complete gratification of his hedonistic needs. Unlike the opiates, it is not in itself a complete mode of adjustment to life; primary needs are not wholly obliterated, an all-embracing sense of well-being and freedom from threat is not obtained, the kick is less rhapsodic, and fantasies are less grandiose and omnipotent. Alcohol is not really a genuine euphoriant. Its chief psychological effect is not inhibition of the self-critical faculty but, rather, release of cortical inhibition of emotional expression, thereby intensifying preexisting mood. Hence, depression may be precipitated as well as exhilaration. There is also a spurious appearance of euphoria because the loss of inhibitory control makes speech and behavior seem buoyant and exuberant. Underneath the overt jocularity, however, may be much sadness and self-depreciation. Frequently the use of alcohol leads to motor incoordination, impairment of orientation, and disruption of higher mental processes. The essentially unaggressive opiate addict may also be particularly disturbed by the belligerency which alcohol generates.

It is true, of course, that genuine physiological dependence develops in the course of alcohol addiction. However, since tolerance is relatively limited, irregularly acquired, and may even decrease after a certain point, since alcohol has little or no effect on smooth muscle or on the autonomic nervous system, and since withdrawal is not invariably followed by pathognomonic signs in tolerant persons, it is difficult to apply the cellular tolerance theory (see pp. 14-16) to the explanation of the abstinence symptoms seen in delirium tremens and other forms of chronic alcoholism. These latter symptoms may be reflective of a gross disturbance of homeostatic equilibrium following abrupt withdrawal of alcohol (see barbiturate addiction, Chapter 6).

Alcohol has more adjustive value to persons who *do* develop mature ego aspirations, but for various reasons of constitution or upbringing, experience difficulty in sustaining them without a crutch. The typical alcoholic finds continuous striving at an adult level difficult and stressful. He needs a crutch, a part-time escape from reality without relinquishing his more mature motivations completely.

Diagnosis

In making a psychiatric diagnosis of drug addiction, using the classificatory scheme elaborated above (see pp. 39-54), we must remember that actual causation is multiple in nature. Addicts are classified in terms of personality predispositions simply because these factors are most differential, distinctive, and diagnostically convenient. But in reconstructing the origin of each individual case, such factors as availability, idiosyncratic experience, and the attitudinal orientation of the culture as a whole, of the neighborhood, and of the peer group must be carefully evaluated. Frequently also, borderline or mixed cases are encountered.

A definitive diagnosis can only be made after obtaining an exhaustive psychiatric history and performing a complete psychiatric examination, which preferably includes one or more projective tests. The history should stress personality development, parent-child relationships, peer-group relationships, school and vocational experience, and characteristic patterns of setting and striving for goals. A detailed addiction history—when and how it began, drugs used, dosage and method of administration, effects of the drug, reasons for using it, attempts at cure, reasons for relapse—is obviously of great importance.

In any case, it is extremely difficult to recognize addicts who are affluent or members of the professional and managerial group. As Jaffe (1970) points out:

> The addict who is able to obtain an adequate supply of drugs through legitimate channels and has adequate funds usually dresses properly, maintains his nutrition, and is able to discharge his social and occupational obligations with reasonable efficiency. He usually remains in good health, suffers little inconvenience and is, in general, difficult to distinguish from other patients.

Chapter 4
Social Characteristics
of
Opiate Addiction

Brief History

The history of drug addiction is both interesting in its own right and important as an object lesson in the ruinous social consequences of uncontrolled addiction. It also provides some illuminating insights into the economic and social factors that favor the spread of narcotism.

The cultivation of the poppy plant dates back to prehistoric times, probably originating in Mesopotamia. The ancient Egyptians and Persians, and later the Greeks and Romans, used opium extensively for medicinal and sometimes for pleasure-seeking purposes. Among Greek, Roman, and Arabic physicians, opium enjoyed the reputation of a panacea, and was enthusiastically prescribed for all ailments ranging from headache to leprosy. From the Mediterranean area, opium was carried to India and China by Arabian traders.

China

More than in the case of any other nation, opium has played a crucial and disastrous role in the history of China over the past 200 years.

> In addition to retarding economic development, opium cultivation and opium profits have corrupted political life and financed civil disorder and revolution. The weak role China has played in international politics, particularly in its nineteenth-century relations with

the Occident and its twentieth-century relations with Japan, has been
due in part to the excessive appetite for opium which existed among
such a large portion of the Chinese people (Merrill, 1942).

For almost the first 1,000 years after its introduction into China
by the Arabs, opium was used solely for medicinal purposes. It
became a household remedy for such diseases as malaria and
dysentery. In the seventeenth century, however, following the
introduction of tobacco into the Far East, opium was frequently
mixed and smoked together with tobacco. Although the original
purpose of this practice was to combat various tropical diseases, its
pleasurable effects soon became apparent, and opium alone was
smoked. By 1729, the habit of opium smoking had become so
widespread that an imperial edict was issued against it. This law,
however, had little effect. The East India Company, controlled by
British merchants, acquired control of the opium monopoly from the
Dutch in 1781 and smuggled increasingly greater quantities of the
drug into China.

Despite a second prohibitory edict, issued in 1800, which forbade
the cultivation and importation of opium, the amount of Indian
opium annually introduced into China continued to increase.
Inspection of Indian ships for contraband on the Canton River led to
armed clashes between the smugglers and the government. Finally,
in 1839, government confiscation of 20,000 chests of opium precipitated the Opium War between England and China. Following this
unequal contest, the victorious English plied the illicit trade even
more briskly, and in 1860 eventually forced the reluctant Chinese to
legalize the opium trade. In the meantime, both because the outflow
of silver currency for the purchase of opium was impoverishing the
country and because the laboring classes could not afford the heavily
taxed Indian opium, domestic production of opium was greatly
increased. By 1900, China produced six times as much opium as
was imported from India.

Oppressive conditions of life for the greater number of Chinese
people, plus little education and opportunity for recreation, facili-
tated the spread of the opium habit. The habit, in turn, which the
poverty-stricken Chinese people could ill afford to cultivate, led to
malnutrition, general debility, loss of earning power, and increased
impoverishment. In many provinces, high poppy acreages resulted

in widespread famine. By 1906, 20 percent of the adult population was smoking opium periodically, and 40 million of these persons were said to be addicted. To add to this misery, England, France, Germany, and Switzerland shipped huge quantities of heroin and morphine into China.

The opium menace was so serious in 1906 that a ten-year prohibition plan was introduced by the government. Embarrassed by public opinion at home, the English government agreed to restrict and later halt the exportation of opium to China. Stringent control and drastic penalties (including beheading) all but wiped out the habit. But, unfortunately, between 1917 and 1934, the authority of the central government declined. The narcotic laws could not be enforced. Corrupt military governors and warlords grew rich on the drug traffic, encouraged opium production, and issued licenses for smoking dens.

Beginning in 1934, when the authority of the central government was restored, a new six-year prohibition plan was launched. Opium became a government monopoly and was sold only to licensed addicts who were simultaneously required to undergo treatment. Cultivation of poppy crops was curtailed, and the death penalty was reintroduced for drug peddlers and incorrigible addicts. But again the prohibition movement was sabotaged, this time by smugglers (especially Japanese) operating from foreign concessions and protected by extraterritorial courts. When open war broke out in 1937, Japanese military governors and their Chinese puppet regimes abandoned all narcotics controls, encouraged the recultivation of poppy crops, and legalized opium smoking in the cities. In unoccupied China, however, the prohibition program continued to function and make headway. According to the most reliable information, stringent law enforcement has all but eliminated opiate addiction in Communist China.

Other Countries

As Chinese laborers and traders emigrated to other parts of the Far East—Formosa, Macao, French Indochina, Siam, the Malay States, the Netherland Indies, and the Philippines—they carried the opium habit with them. With the exception of the United States government, other colonial powers cynically tolerated the practice, establishing opium monopolies that netted huge revenues. At the same time, they strictly prohibited addiction among their own nationals, rationalizing this obvious inconsistency with the absurd pretext that opium did not harm the Chinese. As already mentioned, opium had been introduced into India by the Arabs and was used extensively both at home and for the export trade to China and other parts of the world. Although opiate addiction has long since been outlawed in India, that country is still one of the major opium-producing nations.

The Near East, of course, was the original home of opium. Opium smoking and eating were widespread in Turkey and Persia as early as the sixteenth century. These countries still produce a large percentage of the world's opium output but strictly prohibit opiate addiction. Opium smoking was rife in Egypt prior to World War I; and since that time, although rigidly suppressed, it has been supplanted to some extent by the use of morphine and heroin.

Despite Japanese toleration and encouragement of opium addiction in occupied China and Manchuria, her own citizens and her subject nationalities in Korea and Formosa were well protected from narcotic addiction by strict laws and conscientious enforcement. The opium user in Japan is considered a social outcast, and the rate of addiction in Japan is considerably lower than in the United States.

In Europe, opiate addiction, for reasons difficult to ascertain, never became as serious a problem as in the Orient or for that matter in the United States. As a medicinal agent, however, opium has enjoyed tremendous vogue among the famous physicians of Europe, including Paracelsus and Sydenham. Nevertheless, mild epidemics of opiate addiction did occur following the Crimean War, the Franco-Prussian War,* and World War I. Narcotic laws are strictly enforced in all parts of Europe, except in England, where registered addicts can obtain heroin legally in greater than maintenance doses from certain medical specialists.

Because of the effects of American influences, in part, narcotic addiction has been slowly increasing in Europe in recent years, particularly among youth. According to Battegay et al. (1976),

---

* Hypodermic injection of morphine for therapeutic use first came into general use about this time.

"three general factors seem to be responsible for the drug use among juveniles: (1) the family situation of childhood, (2) the conflicts of norms of the society in which they are involved, and (3) the milieu provocation."

The United States

Drug addiction in the United States has never been the serious national problem it was in China and Egypt. On the other hand, it has been more widespread a disease than in Europe or Japan. During the nineteenth century, exposure to opiates occurred chiefly through the use of patent pain-killing medicines. A new form of mass exposure developed during the Civil War with the introduction of the hypodermic method of administering morphine. Opium smoking itself was introduced into the large cities of the Pacific and Atlantic coasts by Chinese immigrants. The habit was soon adopted by many non-Chinese urban dwellers and became something of a fad. Increased public awareness of the dangers of addiction through opium smoking first led to the imposition of higher tariff imposts. But this only resulted in increased smuggling and in the clandestine manufacture of smoking opium from the less-highly taxed medicinal form of the drug. The Pure Food and Drug Act of 1906 helped to drive many patent opiate remedies off the market by requiring complete and accurate labeling of all drugs. In 1909, the importation of opium, except for medicinal purposes, was banned by Congress.

Definitive control of opiate addiction, however, awaited the passage of the celebrated Harrison Narcotic Act of 1914 and its subsequent amendments. This act restricted the importation, manufacture, sale, and dispensing of opiates to licensed dealers for medicinal uses only. It required the keeping of accurate records and inventories, and made illegal or fraudulent possession of narcotics a criminal offense. Physicians were enjoined from prescribing opiates except for bona fide medical purposes. An amendment in 1930 provided for the establishment of a Bureau of Narcotics to enforce the provisions of the act and to apprehend violators.

There were two unfortunate by-products of the Harrison Narcotic Act. In the first place, more than 100,000 addicts were suddenly cut off from their legal supply of drugs. Treatment facilities were generally unavailable, and continuation of the habit automatically put them in the category of criminals. Thousands of addicts were incarcerated in federal prisons. Second, a huge new illegal narcotics traffic was created. To obtain their drugs, addicts were forced to purchase them at fantastically high prices from the underworld. To correct the first situation, Congress authorized the establishment of two narcotic farms in 1929 for the confinement and treatment of drug addicts, and established a Mental Hygiene Division within the U.S. Public Health Service to administer them and conduct research on drug addiction. The first of these hospitals was opened in 1935 in Lexington, Kentucky. The second problem—suppression of the drug traffic—was handled in part by the Federal Narcotics Bureau and by narcotic squads on the police forces of the larger cities.

Incidence Trends

The exact number of drugs addicts in our midst can never be known. "The drug addict is not easily detected, nor counted" (Goldstein, 1953); and since drug addiction is legally and socially unacceptable, it is obviously to the advantage of the confirmed drug addict to conceal his identity. Estimates based on regional surveys and on reported violations of the narcotic laws are at best informed guesses. Obviously, available statistics on the number of known addicts are minimal figures. Nevertheless, even if the absolute incidence rates are unknown, such figures enable us to ascertain trends.

Immediately following the passage of the Harrison Narcotic Act in 1914, the incidence of drug addiction dropped sharply. The outbreak of World War I undoubtedly favored this trend by disrupting commerce with opium-producing nations. But as is usually the case after modern wars, the postwar period was characterized by a marked but self-limited increase in addiction. One estimate, probably exaggerated, made in 1918, placed the number of addicts at approximately one million. Kolb and Du Mez arrived at a figure of 109,000 in 1924, based on an estimated rate of one addict per 1,000 population. By 1937, the incidence rate dropped to less than one addict per 5,000 population. During World War II, drug addiction characteristically decreased. Since 1948, however, as was anticipated, various indices of addiction have risen sharply. The peak of this increase was reached in 1950. Thereafter the trend, as indicated by the yearly total of narcotic violations for 1951 and 1952 was downward and in the direction of pre-1948 incidence rates.

A special feature of the wave of addiction between 1948 and 1951 was the "alarming increase in the number of young persons, those in their teens and early twenties arrested for violation of the federal marihuana and narcotic laws in New York, Chicago, and San Francisco" (Bureau of Narcotics, U.S. Treasury Department, 1950). In their report for 1951, the Federal Bureau of Narcotics noted that

> the use of narcotic drugs by teen-agers is primarily located in large metropolitan centers; there is little of it in small cities and rural areas. Addiction among boys is almost 10 times as great as it is among girls. Many of the young addicts have criminal records before they come to the attention of the Bureau of Narcotics (Bureau of Narcotics, U.S. Treasury Department, 1952).

Illustrative of this trend was the increase in the number of addicts under 21 years of age in the two government drug addiction hospitals from 22 in 1947 to 440 in 1950. In New York City's Bellevue Hospital, no adolescent addicts had been admitted from 1940 to 1948; however, during the first two months of 1951 alone, 84 cases of adolescent addiction were admitted (Zimmering, 1951). Fortunately, however, as reflected in the decreasing number of adolescent narcotic arrests and in the diminishing number of cases coming to the attention of the Board of Education in New York City (Goldstein, 1953), this teen-age, urban-slum epidemic seemed to be petering out in 1953.

In the sixties and seventies a second more severe epidemic broke out (see Preface to Second Edition). In 1975, the number of narcotic addicts in the United States was estimated to be 450,000, 70 percent of whom were untreated or in penal institutions (De Long, 1975).

From 1968-1972, heroin addicts were older, better educated, and more intelligent than nonaddict offenders. "These findings support the view of the addict being relatively more socially competent than his nonaddict offender peer" (Platt et al., 1976), and of the outgoing, socially facile, and manipulative personality structure of typical (i.e., "inadequate personality") addicts (Ausubel, 1948).

Relevant Factors in the Incidence of Narcotic Addiction

Many attempts have been made to relate the incidence of drug addiction to such social factors as age, sex, race, ethnic origin, occupation, socioeconomic status, place of residence, religion, and educational level. They indicate that in the United States, at least, drug addiction is found in every geographical location, among all occupations, and in every identifiable ethnic, racial, religious, socioeconomic, and educational stratum. However, in most respects, when the social characteristics of a population of drug addicts are compared to those of a nonaddict population, drug addiction largely emerges as a product of the urban slum with its culturally unassimilated racial and ethnic minority groups.* And most of these differences can be explained on the basis of differential access to, or availability of, narcotic drugs and differential community tolerance toward addiction.

The age range between 20 and 34 used to be the most typical period in the life cycle for the onset of drug addiction, including 60 to 70 percent of all cases. As already noted, however, the recent trend has been toward a lower age of onset. The percentage of violators under 25 increased from 18.7 in 1948 to 25.6 in 1949. Today most addicts begin their addiction careers in their early teens. The ratio of male to female addicts varies from 2–4 to 1 in different reports. This sex difference is undoubtedly attributable to the greater exposure of adolescent boys and men to the social conditions under which the drug habit is acquired. More frequently than boys, female addicts come from broken homes (Chambers, 1970) and exhibit more disturbed family relationships (Klinge et al., 1976). Women are usually introduced to illicit drug use by men (Suffet & Brotman, 1976), but also by other women. Although fewer women than men use drugs, on the whole, this difference is

---

* Recent reports from the Drug Enforcement Administration indicate rising incidence trends among women, white middle-class youth and residents of small towns and suburban areas (New York Times, June 19, 1975). In the suburbs, heroin use is primarily spread by deviant peer groups (Levengood, 1973).

steadily decreasing, particularly among younger age groups and among persons committed to "liberal values and a liberal life style" (Suffet & Brotman, 1976). With the increasing rise of feminism, the percentage of illicit women drug users is likely to exhibit a corresponding increase. Typically in the past, most women addicts supported their habits by prostitution. They are now turning more to stealing, burglary, dealing in drugs, and other forms of "hustling" (File, 1976).

Examination of the data relating to other social factors confirms the thesis that socioeconomic conditions affect the incidence of drug addiction primarily by influencing the availability of drugs to those individuals already predisposed on other grounds. Thus, the highest incidence of drug addiction is found among physicians and nurses and in disorganized urban areas with port facilities which offer illicit drug distributors most opportunity for smuggling, a relatively protected and congested market, and personal anonymity. It is no wonder then that the candidate for drug addiction is more likely to live in poor rather than good neighborhood environments, to have an irregular employment history, to be in marginal economic circumstances, and to seek employment in personal service, recreation, and amusement occupations.

Addicts and nonaddicts also differ significantly in their ethnic and racial origins and in their educational status. In comparing the social-class backgrounds of addicts and nonaddicts, however, the disproportionate number of addicts who originate in the lower class can undoubtedly be attributed, in part, to the greater availability of drugs in slum urban areas rather than to lower-class status per se. As pointed out above, however, more lower- than middle-class persons become inadequate personalities.

There is a natural variance in particular geographical localities according to the makeup of the local population. Hence, in relation to national census figures, there are a disproportionate number of Chinese and Mexican addicts on the West Coast and a disproportionate number of Chinese and black addicts in Chicago. In New York City, narcotic addiction is disproportionately greater among blacks and Puerto Ricans. Religious affiliation is not consistently related to rate of addiction, and the geographical distribution of addicts is comparable to the geographical distribution of the population at large. Reflective perhaps of the relatively low incidence of addiction in Europe, the percentage of foreign-born addicts at the Lexington hospital is significantly less than in the general population.

Sociocultural Attitudes

Whether or not an individual first chooses to try and then continues to use drugs depends upon more than personality or developmental predispositions and the factor of availability. Much also depends upon the attitudes toward drugs prevailing in his immediate and wider sociocultural milieu, his own idiosyncratic experience with them, and the changing pattern of relationships between himself and his primary social group as he becomes progressively implicated in their use.* The importance of wider cultural attitudes is immediately apparent when we contrast drug use in China with similar practices in the United States. The relative degree of tolerance exhibited toward narcotism in the first country, and toward alcoholism in the second, roughly parallels the relative esteem in which a passive, contemplative or an active, aggressive orientation to life have generally been held in the respective cultures.

Before he ever comes into contact with drugs, the individual often has an attitudinal predisposition for or against them. This, in general, corresponds to the orientation of his neighborhood or community. In areas where incidence and availability are low, the orientation is almost uniformly negative. Where the opposite conditions prevail, the orientation is more variable, sometimes being extremely negative in one area and highly permissive in an apparently similar adjacent area. *Within* a given neighborhood, however, complete attitudinal homogeneity is seldom found; the individual's orientation is influenced by the values of his peer group, his relationships with peers, and by the identity and relative status of his principal informant.

---

* This discussion, unless indicated otherwise, is based on Stanley K. Bigman's presentation in *Conferences on Drug Addiction Among Adolescents* (1953). For a more recent discussion of sociocultural and personality factors in adolescent drug use, see G. N. Braucht, "A Psychosocial Typology of Adolescent Alcohol and Drug Users," in *Proceedings of the Third Annual Conference of the National Institute on Alcohol Abuse and Alcoholism* (H. Chafetz, ed.). Rockville, Md.: The Institute, 1974.

This provisional orientation, whatever it is, is brought to the initial situation in which an actual choice between accepting or rejecting a shot must be made. At this point, several new factors enter the picture: how prestigious the users are in the candidate's eyes, how dependent he is on their approval, whether they are merely tolerant toward or approving of drug addiction, and the meaning of drug use in the particular situation (sociability, solidarity with group, defiance of adult authority, maturity, or gullibility). With this amount of personal experience behind him, he has a more definite basis for choice. Such idiosyncratic factors as the degree of sickness or pleasure experienced, the occurrence of unexpected gratifications, and the availability of alternative adjustive techniques are extremely important. Equally crucial for subsequent use of the drug are the reactions of his primary peer group to his initial experience—approval or dissapproval, reward or punishment, praise or ridicule (the epithets of "square," "chicken," "yellow," "punk").

If further experimentation with drug use is decided upon, two consequences are inevitable. First, he becomes progressively estranged from the values and standards of nondrug users. He incites the active enmity of his former associates and, in turn, feels misunderstood and abused by them. Second, his identification with the standards of the drug addict world increases. Ties with his former gang and girl friend are broken. He tends to drop out of school and seek the companionship of small groups of users. To guarantee his supply, he tries to make a regular contact with a "pusher." The latter frequently abuses and exploits him (or her) for sexual purposes or monetary gain. But the addict's dependence on the pusher does not permit him the luxury of expressing his hostility overtly.

Both advance knowledge of the properties of drugs and social interpretation of his reactions to them influence the subsequent course of the individual's addiction. Thus, although he may actually be physically dependent on opiates, he may not regard himself as an addict ("hooked") if he does not know about dependence and withdrawal symptoms, and if no one points these out to him as evidences of addiction. The latter symptoms (distress, craving, regular use) may be quite clear, but still uninterpretable in the absence of sufficient knowledge or prior experience. Some aspects of the withdrawal syndrome, especially the faking and the dramatic flourishes, are learned by the neophyte in social situations. On the other hand, accurate foreknowledge of addiction increases the probability of early self-recognition as an addict and, hence, the probability of continuing use. In the absence of such knowledge, the interpretation of his symptoms by others as evidence of addiction serves the same purpose (Dai, 1937; Lindesmith, 1947). Suggestions from others may also modify the actual psychological effects he experiences from drug use and the nature of his withdrawal symptoms.

Even after he decides he is "hooked," sociocultural factors as well as personality needs continue to affect the outcome of addiction. Mere recognition that opiates prevent withdrawal distress and willingness to take "one more shot" for this purpose does not necessarily lead to permanent addiction. Certainly if one only examines the history of permanent addicts, as Lindesmith (1973) did, this sequence of events seems invariable. But the same sequence of events (recognition that opiates relieve abstinence symptoms leading to further drug use) can also be found in transitory addicts, thereby disproving any causal connection between them. Either mature personality needs, strong peer-group pressures, or the availability of adult guidance may reverse the course of addiction after physiological dependence is established.

Crime

Of all the popular misconceptions about drug addiction, the widespread belief that opiate addicts are fiendish and cold-blooded criminals is perhaps the most erroneous and most unfortunate. It is a product of cheap, sensational journalism which makes intelligent and dispassionate public discussion and solution of the problem of opiate addiction extremely difficult.

Most studies (for example, Dai, 1937; Pescor, 1938) of the criminal records of opiate addicts are in agreement that approximately three-quarters of all investigated cases present no history of criminal involvement prior to addiction.* In general, self-reported

---

* The Federal Bureau of Narcotics found that over three-quarters of all addicts have criminal records. Many factors lead to this discrepancy, including: the official bias of the Bureau on this

criminal and drug-taking behavior in addicts tends to be reliable when one allows for exaggerations of dosage used (Amsel et al., 1976). This would seem to indicate that drug addiction is not primarily a disorder which tends to be associated with deep-seated delinquent trends. The figure of 25 percent who *do* have preaddiction criminal records is not excessively high for a population that is largely slum-urban.

Examination of the specific offenses for which addicts are arrested also indicates that opiate addiction does not lead to crime because of the kinds of effects it has on behavior or personality. Addicts seem mainly to break laws in order that they can thereby continue their addiction.* To begin with, the mere possession of narcotics by an addict who cannot produce a bona fide prescription is a criminal offense and the most frequent cause of his arrest. Second, the cost of addiction is so high that few persons could legitimately earn enough to support the habit even if they had the time and inclination to hold down a steady job. Statistics also show that addicts typically engage in nonviolent criminal activity of a remunerative nature, for example, shoplifting, drug peddling, housebreaking, and confidence games. They commit violent crimes typically only under unusual circumstances. Last, although the addict is usually obligated to consort with underworld characters in order to obtain his drug supply, it is highly significant in this connection that once a professional criminal becomes addicted to drugs his associates no longer regard him as reliable.

To appreciate the relationship that exists between drug addiction and crime, one must remember that opiates inhibit aggressive impulses. As will be shown later, marihuana and cocaine have quite different behavioral effects and hence are positively, rather than negatively, related to aggressive criminality.

matter; the overstringency of the Bureau's definition of *criminality,* which includes minor violations implicating most slum-dwelling adolescents; the recording of only drug violators (legally apprehended and sentenced criminals), which would include more criminal types than are found in the USPHS Hospital in Lexington, Kentucky; the inclusion of criminal psychopaths who are not sent to Lexington but are segregated at the Springfield, Missouri, federal prison.

* The annual cost of drug addiction in the United States has been estimated at 10 to 17 billion dollars by the President's Strategy Council on Drug Abuse. More than half of this amount is attributable to treatment of addicts, court costs, loss of earnings from drug-related deaths, and lost productivity (*Knickerbocker News-Union Star,* Albany, N.Y., May 30, 1975).

Proselytism

Opinion differs considerably regarding the extent to which drug addicts and peddlers seek to make converts. In a very broad sense, drug addiction is a "communicable" disease; it spreads by association. However, this does not necessarily mean that addicts or peddlers are active and deliberate proselytizers. Whether or not they are seems to depend on two factors—relationships between supply of and demand for narcotic drugs and the kind of addiction involved.

Prior to World War II, addicts were definitely eager *not* to make new converts (Lindesmith, 1947) since it threatened their own source of the drug, which was in short supply. Peddlers likewise saw no need for marketing campaigns since demand had always exceeded supply, and it was safer to trade with confirmed addicts than with unknown customers who could conceivably be narcotic agents in disguise. But

> as a result of the breakdown in international control of the narcotic drug traffic following World War II, the supply of illicit narcotic drugs [had] risen sharply. At the same time the number of confirmed drug addicts [had] declined. Hence, if a profit was to be made in drugs, new customers had to be found in a hurry. . . . Hard-pressed to create a market, dope peddlers left the safety of the slums, invaded middle-class schools and neighborhoods, and even distributed free samples (Ausubel, 1952).

Proselytism is also more common among adolescents than among older addicts. Here the need for rationalizing their own habits (Zimmering, 1951) and the conformity pressures operating within adolescent peer groups induce initiated individuals to convert their fellows. In addition, because the adolescent addict has fewer means of supporting his habit and less contact with confirmed addicts than his adult counterpart, he is more apt to resort to drug peddling and to a proselytizing type of peddling as a way of financing his addiction.

Illicit Narcotics Traffic

We have already seen that drug addiction would be impossible without the availability of surplus narcotic drugs. It does not require much imagination to appreciate that the primary motivation for creating such availability is the opportunity of making huge profits from the addiction of others. This was the motive behind the large-scale and centuries-long efforts of foreign traders to induce the wholesale addiction of the Chinese people. The same motive today is behind the illicit traffic in narcotic drugs in the United States and other countries. As Col. Frank J. Smith, Chief of the Narcotic Control Section of the New York State Department of Health, puts it: "If you want to know what makes addiction tick, the answer is money" (Committee on Public Health Relations of the New York Academy of Medicine, *Conference on Drug Addiction Among Adolescents,* 1953).

Consider what happens to one kilogram (2.2 pounds) of heroin which can be purchased in Italy for $1,000. Diluted to the strength at which it is sold to addicts, this quantity is sufficient to make 310,000 one-grain capsules, each of which can be sold for $1.00 to $1.50 in New York City (C. E. Terranova in Committee on Public Health Relations of the New York Academy of Medicine, *Conference on Drug Addiction Among Adolescents,* 1953).

Narcotic drugs enter the illicit market through two main channels: the diversion of legitimate stocks intended for medical purposes, and the smuggling-peddling route. The first channel involves the theft of morphine, codeine, and Demerol® from hospitals, pharmacies, and physicians' cars and offices. Sometimes addicts obtain opiates by forging prescriptions and faking serious illness. Physicians and nurses who are addicts simply divert supplies in their possession for personal use.

The first step in the smuggling sequence starts in one of the major opiate-producing nations such as Turkey, Mexico, Burma, etc. Since the amount of opium produced in the world exceeds by four or five times the amount required for legitimate medical usage, international smuggling rings experience little difficulty in obtaining their initial stock. In 1950, 350 tons of opium, sufficient to supply the entire world's needs for one year, simply disappeared from Iran (Committee on Public Health Relations of the New York Academy of Medicine, 1953, p. 199). Divided into small lots, secretion of the drug is relatively easy, as is smuggling it into the country. Big-shot underworld racketeers then distribute it to various middlemen in metropolitan centers until it reaches the hands of the small neighborhood peddler. Only the last-mentioned link in the chain of distributors is typically an addict. To facilitate the unimpeded traffic of narcotics, "protection" is frequently purchased from corrupt politicians, police, and other law-enforcement officials. Hence, as a result of this and other protective devices available to the professional criminal, it is usually only the small-scale peddler rather than the big-time drug racketeer who is caught in police roundups. The apprehension of drug peddlers is further impeded by the reluctance of addicts to reveal and, thus eradicate, the source of their drug supply.

Legal Control

At the federal level, several agencies cooperate to suppress the drug traffic. The Customs Bureau, aided by the Coast Guard, tries to limit the amount of narcotics smuggled into the country. Until recently the Federal Bureau of Narcotics administered the Harrison Narcotic Act and the Marihuana Act of 1937 in addition to combating illegal traffic in drugs within the United States. The Public Health Service is assigned the task of estimating the quantity of opium required for medical purposes. The production of crude opium, the manufacture of heroin, and the importation of manufactured opiates are forbidden in the United States; and the manufacture of opium derivatives and of synthetic substitutes for morphine was carefully supervised and regulated by the Federal Bureau of Narcotics, the staff of which had recently been expanded. Currently the Drug Enforcement Administration of the United States Department of Justice has the major legal responsibility for controlling the drug traffic in the United States but has proved no more effective than its predecessors (Horrock, 1975).

Each of the states also regulates the use of narcotic drugs and controls their intrastate traffic. To do this job most effectively and to eliminate glaring inconsistencies among states, a uniform State Narcotic Drug Act has been adopted by 44 states, the District of Columbia, and Puerto Rico. In addition, many cities enforce local ordinances curbing the illicit traffic in drugs. New York City, for example, maintains a narcotics squad of 100 men within its police department.

At the very best, however, law enforcement can only minimize but never completely eradicate drug addiction. Smuggling can only be eradicated by limiting opium production to the amount needed for medical purposes; but this requires international cooperation. The control of the illicit drug traffic within our borders also requires the elimination of bribery and corruption from local police forces. Finally, the medical profession itself must maintain a high standard of ethics and alertness to prevent the illegal diversion of narcotics from their legitimate purposes.

To combat the rising incidence of drug addiction between 1948 and 1951, many new legislative proposals, some ill-advised and hysterical in nature, were submitted to Congress and state legislatures. The Boggs Law, passed by Congress in 1951, provided for mandatory sentences for second and subsequent violators of narcotic statutes. Several states (notably New York) have enacted similar laws imposing more severe and mandatory minimum sentences for the possession or sale (especially to minors) of narcotic drugs. Such laws have a salutary effect in discouraging the operations of nonaddict peddlers and drug traffickers, but, unfortunately, make no provision for the more lenient handling of addicts who turn to peddling merely to support their own drug habits. Fortunately, legislators have had the good judgment to resist widespread suggestions that drug peddling be made punishable by death. Both California and New York State have extensive provisions for cure and criminal commitment to residential and aftercare treatment facilities.

International Control

The international scope of the narcotics problem was apparent as early as 1909, when the Shanghai Conference was called at the instigation of President Theodore Roosevelt. This first international conference was succeeded by the Hague Convention of 1912, the Geneva Conventions of 1924 and 1931, the Bangkok Convention of 1931, and the Protocol of Paris in 1948. Generally speaking, the same goals, problems, obstacles, and stumbling blocks presented themselves at each convention. Through the years, many costly lessons were slowly learned; and although much has already been accomplished, much more still remains to be done.

The early agreements suffered especially from vagueness, equivocation, lack of universal participation, and absence of enforcing machinery. The participating nations, for example, tried to limit drug use without limiting drug revenue, and to bar prepared (smoking) opium from international traffic without imposing any restrictions on crude opium, which could easily be converted into the former. Each nation was free to interpret the agreements as it saw fit. Instead of putting restrictions into effect immediately, periods as long as fifteen years were set for the elimination of opium smoking in the Far Eastern colonies. These defects were slowly remedied after World War I, when the League of Nations established an Advisory Committee on Opium and Other Dangerous Drugs and a Permanent Opium Control Board. More or less universal ratification of the agreements was achieved, and international supervision of the drug traffic was established.

It was eventually realized, however, that the illicit traffic in drugs could not be halted by administrative control of distribution alone. As long as a tremendous surplus of opium far in excess of the world's legitimate medical needs was produced and manufactured, smuggling was bound to continue. Hence, in 1931, agreement was finally reached regarding the limitation of manufactured opium derivatives. Enforcement of this agreement by the League of Nations gradually reduced the illicit trade in morphine, codeine, and heroin in all parts of the world except the Far East. Japan's former role in subverting these international conventions has already been considered.

Today international narcotics control is divided among three United Nations agencies which estimate the world's legitimate medicinal needs for opiates, enforce existing legislative and administrative machinery for curbing the illegal traffic in drugs, and extend help to individual countries in which addiction problems are severe. The two main unsolved problems are inability to agree on a codification and simplification of existing conventions, and disagreement on a plan to limit the production of crude opium (as well as the manufacture of opium derivatives) to scientific and medical needs.

For one thing, large opium-producing nations such as Turkey* have (unlike India) been unable to find a satisfactory agricultural substitute for their poppy acreage; they are also loath to lose the revenue imposed on opium production and export. For another, buyers (manufacturers) and sellers (producers) of opium are unable to agree on a mutually satisfactory price. Until these two major international problems are solved, American law-enforcing officials are frankly pessimistic about the possibility of drying up the supply of illicit drugs that originates in foreign countries and is smuggled into the United States.

---

* Turkey was persuaded by a United States subsidy in the early seventies to ban the cultivation of the opium poppy. This resulted in a worldwide heroin famine. In 1974, Turkey abrogated the agreement and the world supply of illicit heroin is now rising.

Chapter 5
Treatment
and
Prognosis

Drug addiction is primarily a personality disorder. It represents one type of abortive adjustment to life that individuals with certain personality predispositions may choose under appropriate conditions of availability and sociocultural attitudinal tolerance. As a sick person, regardless of the relatively discouraging prognosis of his disability, the drug addict is entitled to the best treatment that medical science can devise. But quite apart from the moral obligation involved, society stands to profit handsomely from successful treatment by reconstituting the parasitic and predatory addict into a socially productive individual. Treatment of the drug addict also serves the same prophylactic function that it does in relation to any communicable disease. If successful, it eliminates a potential source of infection.

Why Addicts Seek Treatment

Because of the difficulty of obtaining drugs and the illegal status of addiction, most addicts are sooner or later confronted with the problem of undergoing treatment. Statistics relating to the frequency of attempted cures are not very meaningful since many so-called cures consist simply of confinement, with or without treatment, until withdrawal symptoms subside. The distinction between voluntary and compulsory cures is also quite tenuous since it refers more to the patient's formal legal status than to his intrinsic willingness to relinquish the habit. How many cures a given patient undergoes depends on the length of his addiction, his degree of accessibility to drugs, how clever he is in escaping detection, and his motivation for seeking voluntary treatment.

The attitudes of addicts toward drugs are decidedly unfavorable from the standpoint of deriving any benefit from treatment. When questioned regarding their current feelings about addiction, only 27 percent of the addicts under treatment at the Lexington hospital unqualifiedly condemned the practice as harmful. Seventy-one percent thought that drugs were beneficial but not worth the cost of imprisonment or social ostracism (Pescor, 1938). Conventional reasons offered by drug addicts for undergoing voluntary treatment include the desire to improve their health, recognition of the harmful consequences of addiction, and the placation of family and friends. More credible to impartial observers, however, were such *real* reasons as impending arrest, loss of contact with a peddler, lack of funds with which to purchase drugs, and the desire to reduce the dosage of drug (and, hence, the expense) necessary to obtain a "kick." Young addicts undergoing initial treatment may be motivated by guilt feelings or fear of eventual outcome (Zimmering, 1951).

Medical Treatment Versus Criminal Offense

The present legal status of drug addiction as a crime* is socially anachronistic in view of the fact that even among jurists it is almost universally regarded as a disease. The criminal status of the practice was retained because of the mistaken belief that only in this way could compulsory treatment, a drug-free therapeutic environment, and adequate supervision of the released addict be insured. Actually all three aspects of treatment could be satisfactorily accomplished, without making drug addiction a crime, by requiring mandatory treatment for all addicts, including those who voluntarily join treatment programs. Under our present system, no compulsion or control can be exercised over the latter group of patients.

---

* Technically speaking, drug addiction per se is not a crime. But since all drug addicts are guilty of unlawful or fraudulent possession of drugs or of illegal diversion of legitimate stocks for personal use, drug addiction for all practical purposes is a criminal offense.

Many unfortunate consequences have resulted from this legal anachronism. The federal drug addiction hospital and the state intramural facility have acquired an unmistakable prison atmosphere which not only subtly influences the attitudes of physicians and attendants toward the patients, but also focuses undue attention on the security and custodial aspects of treatment. Little hope for attitudinal improvement can be anticipated when society adopts a punitive approach toward victims of a personality disorder and treats them as criminals. The illegal status of drug addiction increases its attractiveness for antisocial psychopaths and for aggressively-minded adolescents temporarily alienated from the norms of the adult world. The social stigma attached to ex-convicts also impedes the rehabilitation of treated drug addicts when they return to the community, and discourages parents from seeking the help of courts and social agencies for their addicted adolescent children.

> Lastly, for the same "crime" of using drugs, a patient may be voluntarily admitted to a federal [or State] hospital (to be discharged on request whether or not he has completed treatment); receive a probationary sentence usually requiring six months' treatment at the hospital; or receive an actual sentence ranging from one to five years. If any offense is to be considered a crime, it is certainly a mockery of justice to base penal punishment solely on the criterion of whether the individual involved has voluntarily confessed his guilt or has been apprehended by officers of the law (Ausubel, 1948).

Need for Compulsory Institutional Treatment

Although coercion, even in the form of court commitment (rather than sentence as a criminal), does have certain undesirable implications, it is necessary to insure the adequately controlled and prolonged treatment required for cure. Because of the drug addict's predominantly favorable attitude toward addiction, he certainly cannot be relied upon either to initiate or to complete treatment voluntarily as long as he is free to search the market for drugs.* Of course, if he does submit to voluntary treatment so much the better. But only 18 percent of the addict population at the Lexington

---

* Of 802 voluntary patients admitted to the detoxification unit of a comprehensive treatment system, 69 percent completed detoxification but only 9.6 percent of these patients sought long-term treatment. (M.A. Sheffet et al., 1976.)

hospital were voluntary patients during the typical prewar period (Pescor, 1938). The average drug addict usually decides upon voluntary commitment because of difficulties associated with the procurement of drugs and not because he is sincerely desirous of being cured. Only 30 percent of the estimated 450,000 narcotic addicts in the United States today are receiving treatment; 80,000 are in methadone maintenance programs, 45,000 are in drug-free programs, and the remainder are in prison or on the street (Horrock, 1975).

Inadequate personalities are extremely reluctant to forego the hedonistic satisfactions associated with drug use to which they have become accustomed. Unless compelled to undergo withdrawal, they frequently leave the hospital at the first sign of distress or ungratified craving. At the present time, despite the criminal statutes relating to drug addiction, only prisoner and probationer patients can be legally detained until treatment is completed. Other voluntary patients remain long enough to lose their physiological dependence and leave immediately afterward, so that they can start anew obtaining their euphoria with smaller doses and at less expense. Still others are not convinced that four to six months of enforced abstinence, medical convalescence, psychotherapy, and occupational therapy are necessary if they are to have a fair chance of rehabilitating themselves and avoiding relapse upon release.

Effective and serious therapy of drug addiction is practically impossible outside of institutions that specialize in the treatment of this condition. Accurate diagnosis and skillful treatment of detoxification from heroin require special facilities and trained personnel which are not available in physicians' offices, outpatient clinics, or general hospitals. If an addict is to be taken off drugs, he must be placed in a controlled, drug-free environment. Since most confirmed addicts are either insincere in their desire for cure or unwilling or unable to resist the temptation of relieving their distress during withdrawal, stringent precautions are necessary to prevent the smuggling of contraband narcotics into the hospital. Because addicts are experts in malingering, chicanery, and subterfuge, responsibility for control measures should not be placed in the hands of neophytes. This, among other reasons (such as lack of compulsion and the need for placating a well-paying patient), adds to the difficulty of treating addicts in private hospitals.

Finally, the regulation of withdrawal treatment requires experienced physicians and attendants trained in the observation and evaluation of abstinence symptoms. In certain cases (cardiac decompensation, tuberculosis, general debility), excessively abrupt withdrawal may result in death. Also, except for mental hospitals, few institutions are equipped to conduct prolonged therapy.

In view of these compelling reasons for compulsory institutional treatment, it is difficult to appreciate the position of various authors (for example, Lindesmith, 1947) who advocate a return to the abandoned system of noncoercive, ambulatory withdrawal treatment in free outpatient clinics or in physicians' offices. Since sincere and serious treatment is manifestly impossible under these conditions (Tennant et al., 1975), this proposal is substantially equivalent to the position of those persons who advocate that the drug habit should be legalized for known addicts. It is argued that this procedure would remove addiction from the category of crime, would allow addicts to lead productive lives and abandon criminal activity, and would abolish the illicit traffic in drugs by removal of the profit motive. The present writer can see little validity in any of these arguments, except for the point that addicts would not be obliged to steal if narcotics could be obtained legally.

In the first place, the label of criminality could be removed from addiction through the simple device of civil court commitment. Second, as already pointed out, there is no reason to believe that the typical drug-satiated addict would lead a socially productive life. Third, the profit motive would *not* be entirely eliminated from the illicit drug traffic since there would still be a market for drugs among new converts. Lastly, legalization, even for confirmed addicts, gives the practice a certain amount of social sanction which would have an unfortunate effect both on potential addicts and on the moral structure of society. It is morally indefensible for society to legalize a vice simply on the grounds that restrictive legislation creates an illicit market and, therefore, provides a profit motive for racketeers. The same argument could be applied with equal validity to prostitution, gambling, smuggling, and black-market operations.

Since addiction is an epidemic disease, spread from one addict to another, it is also difficult to appreciate why so many physicians, psychiatrists, civil libertarians, and social scientists condemn compulsory treatment as punitive and as a violation of constitutional liberties when they so readily accept compulsory treatment of venereal diseases, tuberculosis, typhoid fever, leprosy, homicidal mania, and pyromania. Quarantine and compulsory treatment of disease-spreading individuals are public health measures that date back at least to Hippocrates. And as for the so-called artificialization of institutional treatment, these same persons readily accept simplification of the environment for psychotic patients and oxygen for pneumonia and coronary disease patients. Temporary isolation and compulsory treatment no more commit society to indefinite incarceration of the drug addict than is the case for psychotic, pneumonia, or coronary patients.

Elements of Therapy

Therapy can be best considered in two separate phases: (1) getting the patient off heroin (detoxification), that is, curing him of physiological dependence, and (2) rehabilitating him so that his psychological dependence on drugs is broken and he does not relapse after completion of treatment. The latter aspect of the therapeutic program includes physical rehabilitation, psychotherapy, character reeducation, occupational therapy, and supervised postresidential care.

Physical Dependence

Physical dependence is the least difficult component of drug addiction to treat. It is a "self-limited condition that quickly disappears regardless of and in spite of what treatment is given to cure it. . . . Patients with mild habits respond very well to abrupt withdrawal together with a few small doses of codeine and supportive measures" (Kolb and Himmelsbach, 1938). Patients with stronger habituation are withdrawn gradually. The method of abrupt withdrawal ("cold turkey") in these cases, which is still practiced in prisons, is cruel, dangerous, and unnecessary. Extreme care must be exercised in withdrawing drugs from patients who suffer from pulmonary tuberculosis and cardiac insufficiency.

Methadone is the most satisfactory drug for the treatment of withdrawal since it leads to relatively mild though prolonged abstinence symptoms when it itself is withdrawn.* The patient may first be stabilized on morphine (maximum dose of one-half grain every six hours) for several days to allay his apprehension that he might be subjected to the old-fashioned "cold turkey" treatment. Then, methadone is substituted for about one week and reduced rapidly over a three to four day or week period (Isbell, 1951). Currently, only methadone is used in detoxification. The rapidity of withdrawal and the dosage of drugs administered depends upon the degree of physical dependence.

> This is best determined by Kolb and Himmelsbach's method of quantitative evaluation of the patient's objective abstinence signs several hours following withdrawal of the drug (Kolb and Himmelsbach, 1938), since addicts are all too prone to exaggerate when stating their average dose or detailing their subjective complaints in the hope of receiving a larger-than-necessary quantity of the drug (Ausubel, 1948).

However, when addicts are permitted to regulate, within limits, their own detoxification they apparently use less methadone and seem to be more satisfied (Ragani et al., 1975).

Valuable supportive measures are tranquilizers and soporifics to allay restlessness and insomnia; niacin and thiamine chloride where avitaminosis is suspected; glucose infusions in saline in the event of serious dehydration; and kaopectate and antiemetics to combat diarrhea and vomiting. Care must be exercised to withdraw other sedatives and hypnotics soon after the acute phase of withdrawal, or else one form of addiction is merely replaced by another. Sinequan® is useful in treating the insomnia of withdrawal and is also effective in combatting the anxiety and depression frequently accompanying this condition.

Even under the best conditions, however, withdrawal is a disagreeable experience. Patients become hostile, resistive, and often threaten to leave. Hysterical outbursts are not uncommon, and

---

* A recent comparison between methadone and Darvon® shows that the former was superior in suppressing abstinence symptoms. "Regardless of the therapeutic agent, however, "21-day heroin detoxification [on an ambulatory basis] yields a low rate of heroin abstinence" (Tennant et al., 1975).

suicidal attempts are sometimes made. Excessively rapid withdrawal may precipitate transitory psychosis and long-standing anxiety in detoxified addicts.

Just as important as the pharmacological treatment of physical
dependence, therefore, is

> the necessity for firmness tempered with kindness on the part of the
> physician. . . . Yet despite the need for the establishment of rapport
> and positive transference, the physician only too frequently, even in the
> best institutions, openly displays a cynical, moralistic, and hostile
> attitude toward the addict. He is indifferent to the latter's genuine
> complaints, assumes in advance that he is a liar, and maintains that it
> is a waste of effort and money to attempt a cure. Such an attitude
> must be deplored as . . . contributing toward the resentment and lack of
> personality reintegration that helps pave the way for relapse. In the
> case of the voluntary patient, it leads to his requesting immediate
> discharge (Ausubel, 1948).

Variable results have been reported for the effect of electroshock
therapy and frontal lobotomy in relieving abstinence symptoms.
The former procedure seems to be more effective for this purpose
although both methods are equally efficacious in abolishing the
craving for the drug. But in view of the greater ease, safety, and
predictability of the methadone detoxification method, there is no
clinical justification today for utilizing such extreme procedures in
the treatment of the abstinence syndrome. As a long-term cure for
addiction itself, insufficient data are available for evaluating the
effectiveness or practicality of either method. Lobotomy has an
effect on the self-critical faculty very similar to that of morphine
and could be considered a partial neurosurgical substitute for opiate
addiction. However, although it may render the need for morphine
superfluous, it does not lead to greater motivational maturity or
social productivity, but rather adjustively intensifies a preexisting
personality defect. In any case, it is much too extreme a treatment
for a self-limited condition.

Psychotherapy

Individual psychotherapy has a limited place in the treatment of
drug addiction. It is most promising when administered to the
anxiety and reactive depression group of patients, since the latter
individuals are essentially motivationally mature personalities who

can gain insight into the adjustive functions of the drug and need only learn to substitute more socially acceptable forms of anxiety reduction for drug addiction or to use legal tranquilizers. But where basic motivational maturity is lacking, the insight and changed self-perceptions that psychotherapy can confer cannot completely make up for the deficiency of appropriate experience in playing responsible adult roles.* In such cases, vocational rehabilitation is more promising, and psychotherapy can best be utilized in establishing rapport and positive transference between patient and physician so that the former's resistance to considering a new way of life can be combatted. Practical considerations also call for the very selective use of individual psychotherapy since it has been estimated that 400 psychiatrists would be needed at the Lexington hospital alone (Committee on Public Health Relations of the New York Academy of Medicine, 1953) to provide this service on a routine basis.

Group psychotherapy is more feasible from a practical standpoint but has other disadvantages. Because of the addict's versatile capacity for rationalization, his resistance to gaining insight into the real causes of his addiction, and his peculiar group loyalty, group psychotherapy sessions may be easily transformed into group rationalization sessions. But if the group is skillfully chosen, especially in a therapeutic community, and supervised and directed fundamentally toward the individual motivations, defenses, and adaptations of the patient, beneficial results can be anticipated. At the present time, however, the long-term efficacy of group psychotherapy has yet to be evaluated.

Also to be considered, is the possible beneficial influence of an optimistic and inspirational group milieu. This involves the segregation of patients on the basis of attitude and prognosis so that patients with an optimistic outlook and hopeful prognosis are not adversely influenced by the cynicism and incorrigible attitudes of hard-core addicts who do not desire a cure (Ausubel, 1948).

---

* The limited value of psychotherapy in the treatment of drug addiction is in no sense incompatible with the fact that the cause of the disorder is primarily psychological. A causal agent of a given disease may be so prepotent that direct therapeutic measures may be quite ineffective. For example, surgery and public health measures were until recently more effective than drugs in treating tuberculosis.

Rehabilitative Measures

Rehabilitation is the most important aspect of therapy in drug addiction. Releasing the drug addict after his physical dependence is cured leads almost immediately to relapse (Tennant et al., 1975). But although the importance of this aspect of treatment is recognized in theory, the actual facilities and mode of approach are often inadequate because of deficiencies in appropriations or personnel.

The principal aim of rehabilitation is to develop socially useful needs in the addict and to increase his adaptive resources for satisfying these needs. Only in this way—by creating opportunities for mature satisfactions—is it possible to compete with the known adjustive value of opiates for existing hedonistic motivations. As a result, the addict can be made to feel that he is acceptable and that he has good prospects for productive and satisfactory experiences in the community.

The great hope for rehabilitative therapy lies in the fact that maturation of the inadequate personality is only retarded, not permanently arrested. It may take him 40 years to cover the same maturational ground that others cover in 18 years. Evidence for this belief can be "found in the delayed maturation of certain inadequate personalities who suddenly, in middle life, make satisfactory vocational adjustments, and in the cases of those addicts who make exceptionally good institutional adjustments" (Ausubel, 1952). By means of progressively guided work experience and responsibility, it is possible to develop motivations that are originally absent and thereby to accelerate the process of maturation. In many cases, the "improvement of a marginal vocational adjustment might . . . be the determining factor in providing sufficient normal satisfactions for a drug addict so that he no longer finds it necessary to seek the hedonistic properties of heroin" (Ausubel, 1948).

Because drug addiction disrupts normal habits of working (and in the case of young addicts, prevents their acquisition in the first place), time itself is an important therapeutic principle. Addicts require sufficient time in which to establish new habits of work, recreation, and orderly living before it can be expected that these can take root and compete successfully with drugs. At the Lexington hospital and many day-care centers for addicts, facilities are available for teaching the addict numerous agricultural and industrial occupations. He can further his education in the school department and can acquire avocational interests by participating in library, music, and athletic activities. Movies and religious services are also available.

The full benefit of a program of vocational guidance and training can only be realized if sufficient funds are available to make possible vocational assignments that are directed toward therapeutic and rehabilitative purposes "based on the aptitudes, interests, previous training and future plans of the addict" (Ausubel, 1948). Otherwise, patients are merely utilized to meet the labor and maintenance needs of the institution.

An important part of the rehabilitative program involves the correction of physical defects and the improvement of general health. This not only adds to the patient's employability and adaptive resources but also removes a possible occasion or rationalization for relapsing to the use of drugs.

A cardinal principle in the rehabilitation of drug addicts is the idea that, unlike nonaddicts, they must obtain their motivations retroactively from successful work experience rather than be motivated for such experience in advance. Unlike the case in a nonaddict we cannot wait for an addict to become motivated before expecting him to work responsibility. His personality structure is originally lacking in such long-term motivations, and years of experience in exerting himself only for the sake of obtaining his next "fix" further increases his motivational immaturity and irresponsibility (Ausubel, 1952).

Preexisting motivation is not a prerequisite for treating the drug addict. By all available means, we must expedite the addict's chances of obtaining appropriate work experience although he may be completely unmotivated—even if this means temporarily spoonfeeding him. And, by being successful and obtaining ego satisfactions from such experience, he retroactively develops the motivation to seek more of such satisfactions in the future by playing mature adult roles.* In order to implement this principle it is necessary for counselors temporarily to lower their standards of motivational readiness for work or training in the case of addicts (i.e., not to expect as much of them as they would of non-addicts) and to exploit the slightest spark of inclination for productive activity.

This procedure is the only possible route to character rehabilitation in the unmotivated drug addict lacking ego strength, and is the reason why psychotherapy (which relies principally on insight and changed perceptions) is largely irrelevant in the treatment of drug addicts. Identification with a mature adult authority figure (e.g., a counselor or aftercare officer), particularly an ex-addict who is a living example that drug rehabilitation is possible, greatly enhances the rehabilitative process. The addict can identify with the counselor either in an emotionally dependent sense (i.e., work responsibly largely to gain the latter's approval as a parent-surrogate) or, more independently, use him as an emulatory model. The counselor's role in the rehabilitative process also inheres in his capacity for making demands for or expectations of mature, responsible behavior on the part of the addict—a function which the latter's parents often failed to perform.†

Thus in both senses—as mature authority figures with whom addicts can identify and as sources of pressure for personality maturation—counselors play a crucial role in the rehabilitation of addicts. They also interact with them more frequently and regularly than any other staff members in the treatment center and are more apt to have a personal, two-way relationship with them than the psychiatrist (whose relationship to addicts tends to be chiefly professional and more impersonal). In the case of black addicts, it is important to have black counselors—both because of the distrust and often undisguised hostility with which black addicts regard white authority figures, and because white counselors can only imagine but never *really* know what it means to belong to a black caste in a white society (Ausubel, 1963).

---

* This is the main, generally acknowledged principle underlying behavior modification therapy.

† In our view (Ausubel, 1952b), personality maturation (acquiring a sense of responsibility, frustration tolerance, and executive independence, and deferring immediate hedonistic gratification in favor of long-term goals) does not occur spontaneously, but in response to demands and expectations from parents and parent-surrogates.

Follow-Up Measures

The most glaring defect in the current program of treating drug addiction is the absence of adequate follow-up measures when the addict is released from the hospital and returns to the community. Obviously, many of his original personality predispositions to addiction are still present. When to these are added difficulty in finding suitable employment because of vocational inexperience or job discrimination, the frequent absence of a home, and the influence of his old drug addict associates, it is little wonder that he relapses so easily to the use of drugs. Even before he is released, preparations for his reception should be made in his home community. Contact should be established with relatives and friends, with prospective employers, with his minister and family physician, and with a social service agency. He needs continued psychiatric and vocational guidance and help in finding a job, making new friends, and becoming involved in recreational pursuits. Follow-up studies indicate that the discharged patient with the best prospects for permanent cure is the one who has "a home, employment, and the supervision of not only his probation officer but also a parole advisor" (Pescor, 1943).

Unfortunately, the social follow-up aspects of therapy are impeded by the

> recognition of drug addiction as a crime rather than as a disease. Not only is the released drug addict handicapped by the social stigma of being an ex-convict, but he also does not receive the badly needed social work, psychiatric, and vocational guidance normally given to every patient discharged from a state hospital for the mentally ill. Instead, like other ex-prisoners, he comes under the jurisdiction of federal or state probation officers who are more interested in the formal legality of their charges' pursuits than in their social rehabilitation. Thus, there is some truth in the addict's contention that he is forced to relapse to the use of drugs because of various forms of vocational and social discrimination—as proved by the good work records maintained by certain addicts (without the use of drugs) during the war emergency when the need for manpower abolished many discriminatory practices (Ausubel, 1948).

In 1947, an Addicts Anonymous group was formed paralleling the structure and goals of Alcoholics Anonymous. The latter group has achieved considerable success in preventing relapses to alcoholism by recognizing that they are vulnerable to alcoholism and thus cannot drink socially, and by embracing spiritual values, belief in

God or in a spiritual power "greater than themselves," and reliance on mutual help, self-criticism, and expiation. The efficacy of the addicts' movement has not been nearly as great. It is less successful than the parent movement since opiate addicts generally have less mature personalities than alcoholics and less experience in satisfying basic needs without the use of drugs.

The Role of Physician Attitudes in Rehabilitating Drug Addicts

Psychiatrists, as well as physicians generally, tend to have a strong aversion toward drug addicts and to keep them at arm's length if at all possible—even in institutions devoted to their rehabilitation. They express a cynical ("once an addict, always an addict"), punitive, and unprofessional attitude toward them (assuming in advance that they are all liars, fakers, and thieves, bent on obtaining narcotics fraudulently), and thus often do not give their illnesses proper professional attention.

Of course, there is some justification for this negative attitude toward addicts on the part of physicians.

In the first place, addicts tend to be highly manipulative "con artists" and often do feign illness (e.g., coronary attacks, renal colic) to obtain narcotics from doctors.

Second, addicts commit the ultimate medical sin of prescribing potent addicting drugs for themselves, thereby usurping the physician's professional and legal prerogatives.

Nevertheless, the failure of physicians and psychiatrists to treat addicts' physical and mental disorders appropriately and humanely and to give them the benefit of the doubt that all patients deserve (often turning them away gravely ill from emergency rooms) is antithetical to the best traditions of a healing profession and greatly impedes their rehabilitation. In a sense, this unprofessional and cynical attitude becomes a self-fulfilling prophecy. That is, addicts respond with cynicism and resentment toward physicians who treat them punitively instead of as sick individuals with a psychosocial disorder (who, like all individuals, sometimes develop genuine physical and mental diseases), and become even more resistive to treatment and rehabilitation.

Furthermore, addicts are more often sinned against by unethical physicians than they sin against physicians. The number of physicians who sell narcotic prescriptions to addicts, and who knowingly (for a good fee), prescribe large amounts of Valium,® Elavil,® amphetamines, and barbiturates, in the certain knowledge that they will be used for euphoric purposes, has always been a significant factor in the incidence of drug abuse.

In part, also, the attitudes of American physicians toward drug addicts stem from an irrational fear of and moralistic orientation toward narcotics which generally has little parallel among European physicians. American doctors (in contrast to their European colleagues) typically underprescribe narcotics (particularly codeine), even when they are genuinely indicated as analgesics for painful medical and surgical conditions, in the unfounded belief that a few injections of morphine or Demerol® will result in physiological dependence on these narcotics. Actually, it takes, on the average, ten days to two weeks of narcotic injections, four to six times a day, to induce physiological dependence. Furthermore, unless patients have a personality predisposition toward addiction they typically overcome their medically induced physiological dependence on narcotics without undue difficulty and do not become psychologically addicted.

American physicians and psychiatrists also take a moralistic attitude toward prescribing soporific drugs in intractable cases of insomnia or even in the more transitory situational insomnias. Similarly, they avoid hypnotics in the insomnia of agitated depression, often being reluctant to prescribe such relatively safe soporific drugs as Dalmane® and chloral hydrate to patients whose insomnia does not respond to antidepressants, on the moralistic and specious grounds that these drugs are "habit-forming" (see Chapter 1). So what if they are? Is it better for a patient's insomnia to exacerbate his depression and increase his feelings of desperation in a vicious cycle type of reaction, or for him to become temporarily dependent for a few weeks on a hypnotic? Such dependencies obviously do not last long since most agitated depressions are cured within a few weeks or months by antidepressants or, at the very worst, by electroconvulsive therapy.

Furthermore, unlike such dangerous hypnotics as the barbiturates, Doriden® and Placidyl,® which are now common "street" drugs of abuse, Dalmane® and chloral hydrate are not particularly addictive, do not induce florid states of euphoria, and are not associated with serious withdrawal symptoms. Under the circumstances there is little pharmacological or clinical rationale for not prescribing the use of these hypnotics, when indicated, in depressed patients.

The very same moralistic irrationality is manifested by many American physicians and surgeons who commonly fail to prescribe narcotics in sufficiently high doses to control pain in terminal cases of cancer and in other painful diseases, despite the fact that addiction is obviously an irrelevant issue in the case of terminal cancer patients. The most reprehensible and hypocritical type of moralistic attitude toward drugs, however, is exhibited by some methadone maintenance programs (such as the 39 clinics in the New York City Health Department programs), where the use of all psychotropic drugs—including such hypnotics as Dalmane® and chloral hydrate, antipsychotics, antidepressants, and even such innocuous nonaddicting antianxiety agents as Atarax® or Vistaril®—are categorically forbidden. This is rationalized on the incredible grounds that "patients must be taught to function without a chemical crutch"—as if methadone itself were not the biggest chemical crutch, as well as the most addicting, of all the aforementioned psychotropic drugs. In the meantime, the hands of psychiatrists in such programs are completely tied, since the treatment of mania, depression, and schizophrenia in modern times is unthinkable without the use of psychotropic medication.

Treatment Facilities

Hospital facilities for the treatment of drug addiction are still far from adequate but are much improved over the situation only 40 years ago when drug addicts were commonly given the "cold-turkey" treatment in prisons.

Adult addicts are treated in some state mental hospitals and in the psychopathic wards of some municipal and county hospitals. But, generally speaking, these hospitals are already overcrowded and understaffed, and not equipped to render satisfactory treatment. There are also many drug-free and methadone maintenance treatment centers. Private hospitals are extremely expensive and often provide inadequate treatment under uncontrolled conditions. The hopelessness of treating drug withdrawal without compulsion and stringent security measures has already been discussed.

Adolescents

The problem of providing treatment facilities for adolescent addicts first became acute with the rise in teen-age addiction between 1948 and 1951. Special facilities were deemed advisable for two reasons: (1) contact with confirmed and hardcore addicts, such as are found in the Lexington hospital, could hardly be expected to exert a beneficial effect on the younger group; and (2) the adolescent group contains a larger proportion of benign cases (that is, "reactive" addiction) and individuals with relatively low physical dependence. In New York City, two centers for short-term treatment were established in the psychopathic wards of Bellevue and Kings County hospitals. For more prolonged treatment, state correctional schools had to be used. This was unsatisfactory because of the stigma attached to residence in these schools, and because of the dangers involved in mutually exposing addict and delinquent populations to each other. On the other hand, release of adolescent addicts after three or four weeks of treatment frequently resulted in relapse.

To meet the need for more prolonged and satisfactory institutional treatment, New York City established Riverside Hospital in 1952 on North Brother Island. This was a 150-bed school-hospital facility. Half of the per diem cost per patient was borne by the state. Screened and salvageable adolescent addicts were admitted by mandatory court commitment in noncriminal proceedings. Patients were required to undergo a full course of medical psychiatric, rehabilitative, and postcustodial treatment. The hospital was unusually well staffed by psychiatrists, psychologists, social workers, nurses, occupational therapists, and recreational leaders. A complete school unit was provided by the New York City Board of Education. Discharged patients were compelled to attend a follow-up, out-patient clinic staffed by the same persons providing therapy at the hospital.

In spite of the uniquely comprehensive scope of the treatment offered at Riverside Hospital, statistics on the outcome of therapy have been extremely disappointing. Relapse rates have been over 90 percent (Trussell, 1962; 1969).

Drug-Free Therapeutic Communities

Many voluntary drug-free treatment programs (e.g. Synanon, Daytop Village), most of them staffed and administered by ex-addicts, have sprung up all over the country. They emphasize an inspirational group morale, democratic self-government, group therapy based on confrontation, and progressively guided work responsibility. For the most part, results are difficult to evaluate because of the inadequacy of follow-up records. A recent follow-up study of one drug-free program conducted by an independent evaluating agency demonstrated an abstinence rate of about 70 percent in narcotic addicts who completed the prescribed course of treatment (Romond et al., 1975). Graduates spent less time addicted or in jail and more time employed or in school than dropouts; they were also less legally involved.

Group therapy (confrontation or encounter) conducted in such surroundings is usually more effective than in methadone maintenance settings, but often succeeds in destroying a participant's defenses without substituting anything therapeutically more effective. It must be realized, or course, that not only do many shy and introverted addicts fail to function in a group, but also that many group members have a destructive orientation of enhancing their own egos at the expense of others. Some addicts also, with much justification, regard group therapy as an unwarranted infringement on their privacy.

The New York State Drug Abuse Control Commission claims an employment rate of 67 percent for addicts treated from 3 to 9 months at residential centers and then placed on aftercare status (either drug-free or methadone maintenance). In the writer's experience, the true employment rate is closer to 40 percent.

Methadone Maintenance Programs

In 1965, Dole and Nyswander reported a method of treating heroin addicts by administering 90-180 milligrams of methadone orally over indefinite periods of time.* This treatment is based in part on methadone's greater effectiveness by mouth and its longer-lasting effects (24-36 hours for a single dose) than heroin. Patients are gradually built up to a stabilization dose at which point they are supposed to lose their craving for heroin and are not supposed to experience any euphoria. It is also claimed that this dose "blocks" the euphoric action of heroin. In fact, however, most methadone maintenance patients experience overt euphoria prior to stabilization, and a small but significant percentage afterwards, even though it is subliminal and they rarely acknowledge it (Ausubel, Karsten, and Ausubel, 1978).

Actually the so-called "tissue craving" for heroin described as a "metabolic disease" (Dole and Nyswander, 1967) due to intracellular changes has never been proven. It seems more parsimonious to ascribe the continued craving for heroin in detoxified addicts to the preexisting personality predisposition, to the long-standing habit of meeting all life stresses by injecting heroin, and to returning to the old addict-infested neighborhood (Ausubel, Karsten, and Ausubel, 1978). Adding credence to the latter interpretation is the fact that many addicts in methadone maintenance programs, when deprived of their overt heroin (nonsubliminal) euphoria, turn to the euphoric properties of large doses of alcohol, cocaine, barbiturates, methaqualone, Valium®, and Elavil® (Ausubel, Karsten, and Ausubel, 1978).†

Furthermore, many pharmacologists believe that there is no absolute tolerance for the euphoric effects of opiates (Ausubel, 1966a; Seevers, in Committee on Public Health Relations, New York Academy of Medicine, 1962). Even when maintained at stabilized doses over long periods of time there is good reason to believe that heroin addicts are willing to remain in the methadone

---

* Today the maximum dose of methadone used is 100 milligrams, which from experience has been found to be ample.

† The abuse of Elavil® for euphoric purposes by methadone maintenance patients is attributed by Dr. Peter A. Olivers of Merck, Sharpe, and Dohme to "an excessive adrenergic response since it . . . inhibits the reuptake of noreprinephrine at the axon ending" (Private communication, August 1, 1975).

maintenance program without heroin-induced euphoria because they experience minimal (subliminal) euphoric effects which are licit and free (i.e., relief of psychic tension). And with respect to the so-called "blocking" action of methadone, many addicts learn that if they do not take their methadone one day in advance, and inject a large amount of heroin they *do* experience the typical euphoric action of the drug* (Ausubel, Karsten, and Ausubel, 1978). Tolerance to drug effects, especially cross-tolerance, is always relative both to the dose of methadone and to the dose of heroin used and is never absolute (Ausubel, 1966a).

The initial claims of Dole and Nyswander in 1965 for the success of the methadone maintenance treatment were also grossly inflated (Ausubel, 1966a). On the basis of 22 cases, 10 of which were followed for less than 2 months, and the other 12 for varying periods up to 15 months, they hailed methadone maintenance as just as feasible for heroin addicts as insulin is for diabetics. This claim was given premature national publicity in such national magazines as *The New Yorker* (Hentoff, 1965) and *Look* (Berst, 1965).

Fortunately, later independent evaluation based on long-term experience with the treatment showed that it had pragmatic merit as a treatment of last recourse for addicts who were unsuccessful in drug-free programs (Gearing, 1970). The retention rate of patients varies from 45 to 80 percent, most patients abstain from heroin, approximately two-thirds of the patients are gainfully employed or attending school, and involvement in drug-related crime greatly decreases.† The effectiveness of the program is enhanced when such ancillary personnel as counselors, psychiatrists, vocational guidance specialists, clinical psychologists, social workers, and educational specialists are added to the strictly medical team of doctors and nurses (Gearing, 1970; Proceedings of the Third National Conference on Methadone Treatment, 1970).

---

* Many addicts also double their methadone dosage by using two take-home doses in a single day, in order to experience euphoria. Some patients treated in methadone maintenance programs buy "street" methadone periodically to increase their dosage in order to get "high." Eighty-nine percent of a sampled group of applicants to the Drug Abuse Service Methadone Maintenance Program at the Bronx Psychiatric Center in 1975 admitted using illicit ("street") methadone.

† These figures are grossly inflated by statistical artifacts and defective urine monitoring, e.g., the use of non-randomized, unsupervised samples.

Many methadone maintenance patients report such symptoms as euphoria, loss of sexual drive and interest (but less than when on heroin), weight gain, sweatiness, constipation, urinary retention, and abdominal cramps until they are stabilized. Most of these symptoms disappear after stabilization, but some loss of sex drive, interest, and potency*, as well as constipation, tend to persist. In general, methadone patients can lead normal vocational and family lives while in the program but many complain about the daily or bi-daily visit to the clinic. The desirability of eventual detoxification from methadone is a controversial matter among advocates of this treatment.

The tendency toward polydrug abuse by methadone maintenance patients has already been mentioned. A surprising number of middle-class patients also experience reactive depressions* (Ausubel, Karsten, and Ausubel, 1978). Many methadone patients request premature detoxification because of misconceptions abounding in the addict folklore (i.e., that methadone "settles in the bones").

Methadone maintenance patients were rated as significantly less effective and less responsible than drug-free patients, as less highly motivated, and as more passive and less inclined to undertake adult responsibilities† in 1973 than in 1970 (Brown et al., 1975). They also scored lower on learning and recent memory tests than did drug-free patients (Gritz et al., 1975).

Narcotic Antagonist Programs

A recent but less promising treatment modality involves keeping the narcotic addict maintained on a daily dose of a nonaddicting narcotic antagonist like cyclazocine which precipitates a full-blown abstinence syndrome when patients use heroin. The findings to date are equivocal. Like methadone maintenance patients, addicts on cyclazocine soon learned that they could experience the "high" of heroin by avoiding their last dose of cyclazocine. In addition, this treatment has many undesirable side effects (e.g., severe abdominal

---

* In general, about one-third of the patients in methadone maintenance programs remain passive and unmotivated indefinitely.

† This outcome is largely attributable to the unconcerned and contemptuous attitudes of many clinic personnel toward clients, indifference of the staff, arbitrary and rigid rules, etc. Enrollment in methadone maintenance programs is currently declining, with discharges now exceeding admissions.

cramps). However, addicts treated "contigently" with Naloxone, a narcotic antagonist, were institutionalized less frequently than other addicts and also had "higher complete abstinence rates" (Kurland et al., 1976). Patients entering such narcotic antagonist programs are apparently more highly motivated than patients treated in other programs and remain longer in treatment (Chappel et al., 1971).

Choice Among Treatment Modalities

Because of the marvelously efficient adjustive value of drug-induced euphoria for motivationally inadequate personalities, most addicts lack the motivation and incentive to seek voluntary treatment. Hence, compulsory drug-free treatment through civil commitment procedures, first in a residential center involving graduated work responsibilities and abundant counseling, and then aftercare treatment (including residence in a halfway house) in readjusting to the community, is the treatment of choice. The New York State Drug Abuse Control Commission program is based upon this treatment philosophy first proposed by the author in 1948 and in succeeding publications. Unfortunately, this state program relies insufficiently upon character rehabilitation measures, and such rehabilitation as it does is carried out by inexperienced and unqualified mental health personnel. The intramural program, like in the Public Health Service Hospitals in Lexington and Fort Worth, places undue emphasis on custodial treatment and security in a prisonlike atmosphere.

However, we should not abandon the eminently sound and highly promising approach underlying compulsory civil commitment of confirmed narcotic addicts to character-rebuilding residential and aftercare community centers just because programs, ostensibly based on this approach, have been ineffectively implemented in the past. It still deserves a fair trial, because, of all treatment modalities, it deals most satisfactorily with the basic personality predisposition of most narcotic addicts.

Treatment in a drug-free therapeutic community administered by ex-drug addicts, and relying upon confrontation-group therapy is a realistic alternative only for thick-skinned extroverts who do well in highly structured environments and do not object either to the complete invasion of their privacy or to submission to tough-minded and overbearing authority figures.

Very few "graduates" from therapeutic communities come from institutional settings. Noninstitutional drug-free programs have a very low "retention rate" of clients, and have seldom been evaluated for effectiveness in comparison with control populations. In any case, the very small percentage of "graduates" of such programs tend to drift into similar drug-free rehabilitation programs, as ex-addict counselors, rather than to return to the mainstream of vocational life. In general, halfway houses are no more effective than simple probation measures (Smart, 1976). Drug-free therapeutic communities desperately require the services of trained psychologists and psychiatrists, in addition to ex-addicts, as well as less emotionally traumatizing forms of group therapy than they currently practice (e.g., "encounter" or "confrontation"), as well as less authoritarian types of leadership.

The chief virtue of methadone maintenance programs is that they "buy time" and enable a fair proportion of addicts in such programs to lead normal vocational and family lives, and thus obtain ego-satisfaction (from being socially productive and respected citizens) which can compete successfully with drug-induced euphoria. Nevertheless it is the treatment of last resort because it involves subliminal drug-induced euphoria and should be used for a particular heroin addict only when drug-free programs have been given a fair chance and have failed. It is obviously inadvisable for adolescents or individuals who are not incontrovertibly proven heroin addicts.*

Methadone maintenance programs, as presently constituted, are relatively ineffective (when judged on an overall basis) despite their higher "retention rate" of clients, their better vocational and academic achievement, the lower crime rate, etc. The polydrug abuse pattern, the various techniques for obtaining "highs" on methadone, the large number of apathetic clients who simply take their methadone, etc., have all been mentioned above. In addition,

---

* In some private methadone maintenance treatment programs (and even in some less scrupulous nonprivate programs), persons without a proven history of heroin addiction are often admitted, and then proceed to sell their prescribed methadone, thereby helping to spread primary methadone habits.

they are also dangerous, inasmuch as they are responsible for creating more primary methadone addicts (by diverting their methadone to illicit "street" channels) than they have cured heroin addicts.* More counselors, vocational guidance specialists, and mental health personnel are also required in methadone programs; and to prevent diversion of methadone into the street, no take-home medication should be dispensed. Another possible solution is the use of a longer-lasting (72-hour) methadone, or methadonelike drug, that is presently being tested experimentally.† Only in Ohio and Washington, D.C., because take-home medication is not currently permitted, are methadone maintenance programs not the primary source of "street" methadone.

Current Disillusionment in Drug Addiction Treatment and Research

The recent drastic cutbacks in public funding of drug addiction treatment and research programs are both understandable and regrettable. The average citizen is disillusioned in the efficacy of such programs, and by the evident waste of his tax dollars, when, from his point of view, the addiction problem is as severe now as it ever was. He is unaware of the facts that without such expenditures the addiction problem would be even worse and that the current prospect for "cure" has increased tremendously in the past 25 years.

More rational and efficient approaches to treatment and research could result in even much higher rates of cure than exist today. Thus the cutbacks are shortsighted from a long-term point of view. They will, in the long run, result in an increased incidence of drug addiction, and the tax money saved will be more than offset by the increase in drug-related crime. The treatment of more addicts by more efficient methods, on the one hand, would both decrease the incidence of drug addiction and of drug-related crime. And, more

---

* A large, though undeterminable percentage of former heroin addicts in nonprivate (i.e., publicly supported or voluntary hospital clinics) methadone programs sell half of their methadone dosage as a means of supporting themselves. This is the main source of "street" methadone, and of primary methadone habits, which now cause more narcotic-related deaths than heroin habits.

† This drug, known as LAA7, is currently being tested at the Addiction Research Foundation in Palo Alto, California, by Dr. Avram Goldstein and at the San Francisco General Hospital by Dr. J. Arthur Weinberg and Dr. William Hargreaves.

honest and efficient law enforcement would greatly decrease the availability of illicit narcotics, and thereby lower the incidence of addiction, as, for example, during World War II and in postwar China.

Prognosis

It would be extremely unrealistic not to concede at the outset that the prognosis for the cure of drug addiction is guarded at best. On the basis of results of treatment to date, an expectancy of cure in 75 percent of the cases would be optimistic indeed (Horrock, 1975). This is hardly surprising when we consider the tremendously efficient adjustive value of opiates for inadequate personalities. For such persons there are few conceivable adjustive setups which our culture or any culture could dream up that could compete with narcotic drugs in attractiveness. But although the inherent difficulties in the therapeutic situation should serve to keep our aspirations realistic, they should not give rise to defeatism or despair. Despite the generally unfavorable prognosis, "many of the apparently hopeless cases are so only because of inadequate treatment, improper management under treatment, or the unfavorable environment to which [drug addicts] are eventually returned." Nevertheless, it is quite apparent that good prevention may be the best means of treating drug addiction.

Court-ordered commitments have a better prognosis than voluntary cases (Aron & Dailey, 1976; Vaillant, 1963). The therapeutic success of women is more associated with psychologically oriented concerns, whereas the success of men in completing treatment programs is influenced more by sociological factors. The reason for this apparent paradox is that involuntary patients are obliged to submit longer to the prescribed treatment.

Rate of Relapse

Statistics regarding rate of relapse in treated drug addicts are difficult to interpret because the addiction status of such persons cannot be easily ascertained. When a drug addict is readmitted to the hospital, there is little doubt about the fact that he has relapsed. On the other hand, failure to be readmitted does not necessarily mean that he is still abstinent. For this reason, available statistics on rate of relapse are probably minimal estimates of the truth. They explain the occasions, if not the reasons, for relapse.

The largest follow-up study of addict patients released from the Lexington hospital indicates that "excluding the dead and unknown, 74.7 percent have relapsed to the use of drugs and 13.5 percent are still abstinent" (Pescor, 1943). Vaillant (1963) reported a relapse rate of over 90 percent in New York City addicts released from the Lexington hospital. This rate was inversely proportional to length of stay in the hospital. These figures correspond closely to the percentage of recidivism reported at Bellevue Hospital and the State Narcotic Hospital at Spadra, California, which in 1930 was 88 and 85 percent respectively. The average length of abstinence reported in the literature varies from one to three years. At the Lexington hospital, it is 2.2 years after a voluntary cure and 1.8 years after an involuntary cure (Pescor, 1938). These averages, however, are inflated by a minority of relatively long abstainers, since about half of the released patients make no attempt whatsoever at abstinence, 20 percent relapse within the first month, and an additional 6 percent relapse between the second and sixth months (Pescor, 1943). Most methadone treatment programs and the New York State Drug Abuse Control Commission report "cure" rates approaching 65 percent. The graduates of some drug-free programs also approximate this figure (Romond et al., 1974); the dropout rate in such programs, however, is extremely high.

Causes of Relapse

The causes of relapse following treatment may be divided into three general categories: original personality predispositions, personality changes resulting from addiction, and environmental pressures confronting the released drug addict. It is self-evident that even optimal therapy can never *completely* overcome such strong predispositions to drug use as immaturity of goals and goal-seeking patterns and incapacity to meet the demands that the culture makes on mature adults. Having once discovered that the use of opiates is a simple and almost effortless way of satisfying his basic hedonistic needs and enhancing his self-esteem, the addict undergoes additional changes in personality structure. "The individual who has had experience with such drugs is therefore no longer the same as he was before addiction, and he is more predisposed to relapse after each successive drug experience (Wikler, 1953).

As already pointed out, prolonged use of opiates results in the weakening of both primary and socially derived drives and of other drive-satisfying and adjustive techniques. Drug use becomes the preferred, and soon the only adequate, means of gratifying the addict's needs, as well as an important need in its own right.* Its distress-reducing value becomes generalized to include all situations giving rise to discomfort and emotional stress. These acquired needs, memory associations, and adjustive habits easily outlast the addict's physiological dependence. He cannot simply forget that merely by inserting a needle under his skin he can procure instantaneous satisfaction. Even the reaction of physiological dependence and

> the practically inevitable occurrence of withdrawal symptoms almost seem to be welcomed because of the renewed possibility of experiencing the relief afforded by the drug in this situation. This is comparable to the well-known example of the individual who [purposely] knocks his head against the wall because it feels so good when he stops (Ausubel, 1948).

Wikler (1953) suggests the possibility that " 'conditioning' phenomena may play an important role in the genesis of relapse." He points out that postaddicts may experience withdrawal symptoms merely by being present in an environment where drugs are available. The conditioned stimuli here are presumably various cues associated with drug use that formed part of the total situation in which withdrawal customarily took place.

Another concomitant of addiction that increases the possibility of relapse is the favorable beliefs and attitudes about drugs that addicts develop. During the course of becoming addicted, they come to believe that opiates are valuable for just about every ailment afflicting mankind, and gradually tend to lose whatever moral compunctions thay might have originally entertained about drug use (Lindesmith, 1937). Relapse also provides an opportunity for "getting even" with persons responsible for instituting undesired withdrawal (Wikler, 1953).

---

* This discussion applies primarily to the inadequate personality and only secondarily to the anxiety, neurotic, and reactive depressive.

Lastly, environmental pressures generated by addiction itself help drive the released drug addict on the road to relapse. Back in his home community, a social outcast, frequently with no home, and doubtful prospects of finding legitimate employment, he easily falls under the influence of his former addict associates. The first step toward resumption of addiction is almost invariably precipitated by renewed interpersonal contacts with drug users (Dai, 1937; Pescor, 1938). Other reasons for relapse offered by addicts include relief of pain, need to sober up from alcoholic hangovers, desire to experience "just one more thrill," and various forms of environmental stress (Pescor, 1938).

Factors Influencing Prognosis

In estimating a given addict's chances for successful cure, the following favorable prognostic indicators should be borne in mind: (a) a diagnosis of reactive addiction, anxiety neurosis, or reactive depression, as against inadequate personality; (b) beliefs that drugs are harmful or are not worth the risks they entail; (c) no preaddiction record of delinquency; (d) hospitalization in a drug-free environment for a period of four to six months; (e) satisfactory institutional adjustment accompanied by future plans to return to a job and a home; (f) evidence of personality reorganization involving newly acquired goals and interests; (g) the actual availability of a home, employment, and supervision following discharge from the hospital; (h) implantation in a different social milieu and avoidance of former addict associates. Intrinsic desire for cure is probably an important factor, but this cannot be inferred from the patient's formal legal status as a prisoner or volunteer. The favorable prognostic significance of all of these factors, except for the first, has been substantiated by research findings (Pescor, 1943; Vaillant, 1963). In all probability, however, differential personality structure is the most important single prognostic factor, and its relationship to abstinence following treatment deserves the future attention of clinical research workers.

Chapter 6
Addiction
To Nonopiate
Drugs

In this chapter we shall discuss addiction to several common nonopiate drugs. Of the depressants, only marihuana and the barbiturates will be considered. Reference has already been made to alcohol. The stimulants include cocaine, the amphetamines, and mescaline. The use of mescaline is largely limited to Indians in Mexico and in the southwestern portion of the United States. LSD, a hallucinogen, was widely used in the youth culture in the late sixties. No attempt will be made to discuss these nonopiate drugs definitively. Our main purpose in considering them here is to compare them to the opiates with respect to pharmacological actions, psychological effects, adjustive value, and personality characteristics of users.

Marihuana

Extent of Addiction

Marihuana is habitually used by millions of persons throughout the world for the psychological effects it induces. For the most part, the consumption is clandestine in nature and is supplied by illicit traffic. The marihuana habit is particularly prevalent in India, Burma, Egypt, North Africa, Mexico, and the United States. In 1937, 14 percent of the population of Egypt were said to be habitual users. In Europe, the habit is relatively rare and of recent origin.

Although Syria is the world's largest producer of marihuana, consumption in that country is not large.

Marihuana has been extensively used in India as a household remedy, in connection with religious and social customs, and for its euphoric, intoxicant, and supposedly aphrodisiac properties. During the past 40 to 50 years, however, it has fallen into disrepute and is now used mostly by the lower strata of society to combat fatigue and monotony and to generate a sense of well-being. Tightened government control has restricted the incidence to between 0.5 and 1.0 percent.

In the United States

Marihuana use was practically unknown in the United States prior to 1930, except among Mexican laborers in the Southwest. Since then, usage has spread to all parts of the United States, particularly among teen-agers in the urban slums and colleges. Most of the marihuana illicitly used in the United States is smuggled into the country from Mexico, although there is some illegal domestic cultivation. One of the difficulties in controlling the habit is that the plant grows wild in the Southwest and can be cultivated in any part of the country.

The spread of marihuana addiction has been attributed to its constituting a very adjustive type of fad for aggressive, status-starved adolescents in slum areas who are revolting against the standards of conventional society and against the special socioeconomic, racial, and ethnic deprivations to which they are subjected. Marihuana is better adapted to teen-age abuse than opiates, since it is more available, cheaper, and considered less dangerous. For two to six dollars a day (fifty cents to one dollar per cigarette) the marihuana addict can completely satisfy his appetite for the drug. An undetermined number of American soldiers stationed in India and Burma during World War II were also exposed to the habit for the first time.

Coincident with the teen-age epidemic of opiate addiction in 1950 and 1951, the number of marihuana violations also increased. The, peak incidence, however, came a year earlier (in 1949), and the increase was less pronounced. Afterwards the trend was in a downward direction (Bureau of Narcotics, Treasury Department, 1949-

1953). During this same epidemic period a large number of adolescent heroin addicts were introduced to opiate use via marihuana. Narcotic peddlers commonly sold both drugs. Now marihuana is used by youth almost as commonly as alcohol in social situations. In Vietnam, the incidence of heavy marihuana use varied from 30 to 50 percent of American soldiers, being utilized as a coping mechanism to control anxiety and depression (Casset et al., 1968; Stanton, 1970).

Associated Social Factors

Like opiate addiction marihuana use in the United States is largely a phenomenon of youth and young adults. The majority of users start the practice during adolescence; some begin in preadolescence and in their early twenties. As in India, the overwhelming proportion of users are male (although the proportion of female users is steadily increasing) and are inhabitants of deteriorating urban areas. The habit has spread very rapidly among persons in the entertainment field; among jazz musicians, it is almost considered an occupational hazard. The incidence among black and Latin American youth is disproportionately great. The vast majority of cases reported in the Army has been among blacks. This can be explained by the greater incidence of poverty, slum residence, and socioeconomic discrimination among blacks, and by the high status which black jazz musicians enjoy among members of their race. The black youth also resents the submissive role in which the prevailing white stereotype casts him.

> Marihuana, insofar as it removes both anxiety and submission, and, therefore, permits a feeling of adequacy, enables the Negro addict to feel a sense of mastery denied him by his color. The white psychopath or neurotic not faced with a dual problem of personality and environmental frustration finds alcohol or other forms of satisfaction more acceptable (Charen and Perlman, 1946).

Unlike opiate addicts, marihuana users are avid proselytizers and prefer to enjoy the effects of the drug in large social gatherings ("tea parties").

Casual or recreational use of marihuana is an incomparably more common phenomenon than is the case with opiates. Addicts tend to associate with other addicts and to avoid the company of nonaddicts.

Recognition is established through the use of an esoteric argot and handclasp.

The vast majority of illicit adolescent drug users also use other drugs, both licit and illicit, in addition to marihuana. "The use of illicit drugs other than marihuana rarely takes place in the absence of marihuana use," and "the more often an adolescent has used marihuana the more likely he or she is to have used each of the other drugs" (Single, Kandel, and Faust, 1974). The adolescent typically begins his drug involvement with beer or wine, progresses to cigarettes or hard liquor, then tries marihuana, and finally samples other illicit drugs (Kandel and Faust, 1975). Women marihuana users also tend to smoke tobacco more heavily and to use more alcohol (Rouse and Ewing, 1973). Marihuana use is also positively correlated with left-wing politics, social attitudes, and a generally permissive attitude toward the use of mood-altering drugs (Kohn, 1978).

The gregarious habits of marihuana users play an important role in the establishment of addiction since the proper smoking of marihuana for pleasure is not easily learned. The novice learns from more experienced users how to smoke so that he obtains and perceives the pleasurable effects of the drug. The initial effects (nausea, vomiting, anxiety, depression, fear of death) are often disagreeable until he learns to control the dosage and define its effects as enjoyable. These initial experiences would ordinarily tend to discourage further use were it not for reassurance furnished by associates (Becker, 1953; Goode, 1970).

"In any case involvement with other drug-using adolescents [particularly best friends] is a more important correlate of marihuana use than parental use of psychoactive drugs or alcohol" (Kandel, 1974).

"The search for pleasant sensations, the desire for expanded creativity, and the belief that one would cease taking drugs if they were conclusively shown to be harmful, were more powerful predictors of polydrug involvement [in high school students] than ... socio-cultural factors" (Kamali and Steer, 1976).

Brief History

Indian hemp has been known to man for at least 3000 years before the Christian era. It was first used for such commercial purposes as the production of rope and textiles. It is mentioned in ancient Sanskrit literature dating from 2000–1400 B.C. Later it was utilized for medicinal and anesthetic purposes by Chinese, Hindu, and Arab physicians. Not until the tenth century of the Christian era was it extensively used for its intoxicant and euphoric properties in India and the Arabic countries. The people of Europe were familiarized with the drug through the writings of various romanticists during the nineteenth century.

The numerous names attributed to the drug are somewhat confusing. Commercially and popularly, it is known as Indian hemp. Hashish is the Arabic name and *Cannabis indica* the pharmaceutical term. Marihuana (also spelled *marijuana)* is the official term in the United States. It is variously described as a corruption from the Portuguese *mariguano,* meaning intoxicant, and as a slang word of Mexican-Indian origin. Marihuana cigarettes are referred to as reefers, sticks, and weeds. Three forms of the drug, *ganja, charas,* and *bhang,* are used in India.

Narcotic preparations of marihuana are derived from the resinous exudate of the dried tops of female plants at or shortly after the period of flowering. Botanically, the plant belongs to the genus *cannabis,* species *sativa.* Marihuana refers to the upper leaves or flowering tops and *hashish* to a special form of the concentrated resins. The active ingredient of the drug, which varies in potency depending upon local differences in the species, has been discovered and synthesized within the past fifteen years. The plant was originally indigenous to Central Asia but is now found all over the world, cultivated or growing wild. Hemp fibers are used in the manufacture of twine, rope, bags, and clothing. The seeds are used for making paint, varnish, and linoleum, and in birdseed mixtures.

Control

The Marihuana Tax Act of 1937 placed the same type of federal controls over the production, sale, transfer, and use of marihuana as the Harrison Narcotic Act accomplished in relation to the opiate drugs and cocaine. The registration and tax provision of the act have the effect of restricting the lawful use of marihuana to legitimate medical and scientific purposes. Under the provisions of the Act of 1929 establishing two federal narcotic farms, marihuana addicts were admitted to the Lexington and Fort Worth hospitals. State control of the marihuana habit was provided for by including the drug under the provisions of the Uniform Narcotic Drug Act passed by most states. Since marihuana is explicitly mentioned in the Geneva Drug Convention of 1925, it is brought under the same trade restrictions as cocaine and the derivatives of opium (Merrill, 1950), and comes under the jurisdiction of the narcotic regulatory bodies of the United Nations.

Physical Effects

Marihuana acts almost entirely on the central nervous system. Initially there is an apparent stimulation and exhilaration which is followed by sedation, depression, drowsiness, and sleep. The net effect of the drug is a depressant one, despite a variable degree of initial cerebral excitation. Characteristically, the effects of marihuana are extremely variable and unpredictable. To some extent, they depend upon the personality of the user, dosage, route of administration, and the particular preparation of the drug used. Marihuana may either be smoked or taken orally as a cake of the concentrated resins. By mouth, the effect is milder and more prolonged. In the United States, the drug is almost invariably smoked. The cigarettes look homemade and are often wrapped in brown paper. The customary dosage is three to six cigarettes daily.

The immediate neurophysiological effects of the drug are clumsiness, incoordination, and frequently ataxia, as well as partial anesthesia of the skin, flushing of the face, and pupillary dilatation. Pulse rate and blood pressure are elevated in the early phases. Hunger and appetite (particularly for sweets) are increased, although, in beginners, nausea and vomiting are not uncommon. The frequency of urination is increased, but since the total volume of urine excreted is not appreciably raised, it is not a genuine diuretic. All of these latter effects are interpreted as manifestations of cerebral excitation, the impulses from the cerebral cortex being transmitted through the autonomic system.

Medically, marihuana is rarely used today. It has been employed in the treatment of anorexia, glaucoma, terminal cancer, depression, and the abstinence symptoms of morphine addiction. But since it has no indispensable uses, and since its effects are so unpredictable, most physicians no longer think of marihuana as a therapeutic agent.

The bulk of the clinical evidence indicates that, if tolerance exists at all, it is extremely limited and occurs in only some users. Most addicts continue to obtain the desired effects without increasing dosage. If some tolerance is acquired, it does not persist very long after the drug is discontinued. Animals show no decrease in sensitivity or responsiveness after prolonged use. These data are in accord with the finding that, although sometimes claimed, physiological dependence or abstinence symptoms have never been unequivocally demonstrated.

On the other hand, there is little doubt that the drug is habit-forming or addicting. Despite the claims of heavy users that they can voluntarily discontinue use at any time without experiencing undue suffering or craving, their behavior indicates otherwise. When they anticipate separation from their source of supply, they take steps to accumulate sufficient reserves to "tide them over." Confirmed users bitterly resent deprivation and readily admit their future intentions to return to the drug as soon as conditions permit. According to one study, enforced deprivation results in "anxiety, restlessness, irritability, or even a state of depression with suicidal phantasies, sometimes self-mutilating actions or actual suicidal attempts" (Gaskill, 1945). These symptoms of *psychological* dependence are undoubtedly less pronounced and perhaps even completely absent in casual or recreational users.

No unequivocal evidence of permanent physical damage or deterioration resulting from chronic use of marihuana has been reported in the United States.* In India, on the other hand, where stronger preparations are used and chronic addiction is more common and of longer standing, reliable evidence of damaged health has been reported for 42 percent of chronic users. Among the more typical symptoms are congestion of the eyes, pharyngitis, laryngitis, chronic bronchitis, loss of weight, diarrhea alternating with constipation, and depression of sexual activity. (Chopra and Chopra, 1933,

---

* Evidence on this point is equivocal. Nahas (1975) claims that chronic marihuana use causes impairment of cellular-mediated immunity, chromosomal damage, impotence, a lowered sperm count, bronchitis, laryngitis, and asthma. The Center for Studies on Narcotic and Drug Abuse denies or minimizes these effects (*New York Times,* July 9, 1975).

1942.) The intravenous use of marihuana leads to dangerously toxic symptoms (Payne and Brand, 1978).

Psychological Characteristics of Users

Marihuana users may be classified under the same etiological headings used for opiate addicts. The *primary* group includes those individuals for whom the drug serves an important adjustive function, that is, inadequate personalities, anxiety neurotics, and depressives. The *symptomatic* group consists mainly of aggressive, antisocial personalities in whom marihuana smoking is merely one relatively minor manifestation of pervasive illegal trends. The *reactive* group is made up of essentially normal teen-age youths who respond aggressively to the status deprivation of adolescence as aggravated by particular socioeconomic, racial, or ethnic factors. Recreational users are found in all three categories. Habitual users are most frequently inadequate personalities.

A separate category might be created for the relatively rare individuals who use the drug solely for its presumed musical effects or in connection with premeditated criminal activity. The following description of the more serious types of heavy, chronic, or habitual marihuana user obviously does not apply to the more commonly encountered moderate, part-time, or recreational "social" user.

The Inadequate Personality

The typical heavy and habitual user of marihuana (who is almost constantly "stoned"), and who gets "stoned" regularly and frequently enough to be vocationally nonfunctional, may be described clinically as an immature, emotionally unstable individual, unable to meet the demands of reality or to endure deprivation, frustration, and discipline. He reacts to conflict with either explosive aggression or a need for immediate hedonistic gratification. Characteristically, he comes from a poverty-stricken, broken home or a home marked by domestic strife. A striking feature of his home background is the contrast between a mother with high and exacting moral standards and a morally lax father. Frequent nightmares, enuresis, and other symptoms of emotional tension and disturbed interpersonal relationships are typical of his early childhood history.

Signs of motivational immaturity appear early. His school attendance is irregular and his academic achievement is considerably below the expectancy level indicated by his intelligence. Gambling, sexual promiscuity, and fighting with his teachers characterize his early adolescence. After he leaves school, he shows little inclination for regular employment. He changes jobs frequently, is often unemployed, and pursues a nomadic existence. Preoccupation with sexual gratification is a central component of his goal structure. His record in military service is particularly unsatisfactory. Shirking of duty, insubordination, frequent breaches of discipline, and disruption of morale typify his performance in the armed forces.

Marihuana has adjustive value for these individuals because it generates a sense of well-being and adequacy and restores damaged feelings of self-confidence. It releases aggressive and erotic trends and reduces anxiety connected with socially unacceptable hedonistic gratifications.

The inadequate personality who uses marihuana habitually is similar in most respects to his opiate-addict counterpart. The essential difference seems to be in the fact that he comes from a home marked by greater emotional conflict and by the presence of dichotomous moral traits in the two parents. His typical adjustive response to this home situation is an accentuation of aggressive and hedonistic (especially erotic) trends. The unique adjustive value of marihuana in such cases inheres in its ability to release and enhance these trends. Opiates are unsatisfactory because they depress aggressive tendencies and sex urges. The inadequate personality who turns to the opiates, therefore, must be primarily concerned with attaining the nonspecific psychological aspects of euphoria —the aspects that are realized by inhibition of the self-critical faculty and by elimination of primary drives. The marihuana user, on the other hand, is more actively concerned with experiencing the sensuous and hedonistic components of drug-induced euphoria.

Habit Theory

Paralleling Lindesmith's habit theory of opiate addiction, Becker (1953) has proposed a similar theory to explain the origin or basis of

marihuana use. Becker also dispenses with personality predispositions. All necessary motivations for drug use are supposedly
acquired during the course of learning how to smoke marihuana for
pleasure. Thus, to become a habitual marihuana user, the
individual must only learn to smoke the drug properly, to "recognize
the effects and connect them with drug use," and "to enjoy the
sensations he perceives."

It is self-evident that this theory also fails to account for the
selective incidence of addiction. Without even considering the personality structure of marihuana users, it summarily dismisses this
variable as irrelevant. Like Lindesmith's theory, it proposes that
only one kind of motivation can underlie drug addiction. Clearly
many different motivations can operate simultaneously in this situation. Because learning how to smoke marihuana for pleasure
engenders additional motivation to continue smoking, we are not
required to abandon the proposition that, in some chronic users,
predisposing personality defects (for which the drug is adjustive)
furnish the original motivation.

Lastly, to claim that habits are established because they are
pleasurable is a tautology and a truism that explains nothing. What
needs explaining is not why individuals who find a habit pleasurable
continue to practice it (since this is self-evident), but why only
certain individuals are able to find it pleasurable in the first place,
and why only a minority of those who do enjoy it continue to
practice it. Because a certain sequence of events (namely, learning
to smoke marihuana pleasurably, and continued use of marihuana)
is found in marihuana users, the two events are not necessarily
related causally, nor is the antecedent event the essential causal
factor. This sequence of events would, by definition, have to be
present in all persons who continue to use the drug. Since Becker
naturally found it in all *users,* he uncritically assumed a cause-and-
effect relationship. What he neglected to consider—because *all* of
his subjects were active users—were the cases of individuals who
learned how to smoke the drug pleasurably but abandoned use
because smoking served no adjustive purposes or because other
drugs (for example, alcohol, heroin) were found to be more
adjustive.

In the origin of complex behavior patterns, it is futile to look for single causes. An individual becomes a marihuana addict because he suffers from a personality disturbance for which marihuana is adjustive. But at the same time the drug must be available, there must be some attitudinal tolerance toward the practice in his social milieu, he must learn how to smoke so that the desired effects are produced, and he must have available a source of reassurance to overcome his initial disturbing experiences.

Psychological Effects

The psychological effects of marihuana are both extremely varied and variable in nature. Mood, perception, judgment, and behavior are all affected. The unpredictability of the drug is in part a reflection of the fact that, like alcohol, it "does different things to different persons." Its effects on mood, for example, vary from extreme elation and exhilaration to depression, reverie, panic, and fear of death. More typically, however, it generates a sense of well-being, relaxation, exultation, and inner joyousness. Anxiety and emotional tension are reduced. The self-critical faculty is inhibited, consciousness of inadequacy is lowered, and self-confidence is enhanced.

> Under the influence of marihuana the basic personality structure of the individual does not change but some of the more superficial aspects of his behavior show alteration. . . . The disinhibition which results from the use of marihuana releases what is latent in the individual's thoughts and emotions, but does not evoke responses that would be alien to him in his undrugged state (New York City Mayor's Committee on Marihuana, 1944).

Experimental studies of marihuana users tend to be misleading because the "typical" subject in such studies is not really a "typical" user. Not only is the marihuana experience verbally definable, but it varies also with prior expectancies and experience (Adamec et al., 1976).

Perceptually, marihuana reduces pain and touch sensibility and sometimes induces striking illusions and hallucinations. The distortion of time perception is especially marked. Time appears to pass more slowly; minutes may seem like hours. Near objects may appear distant. The individual's head may feel swollen and his legs light and lengthened. Sometimes, in this dreamy state of consciousness, there may be an illusion of dual personality. If hallucinations are present, they are vivid and pleasant.

Intellectual functioning and judgment are characteristically impaired by the drug as shown by tests of mental ability. Fantasy and imagination are stimulated, and ideas are plentiful but disconnected and disorganized. Behavior is boisterous, uninhibited, impulsive, hilarious, and silly. The marihuana user is voluble and garrulous. He does much giggling and laughing over pointless jokes. In social gatherings, he may vie with other users to see who can be most ridiculous and repulsive. At times, aggressive, irritable, and irresponsible behavior may result. Transient toxic psychoses characterized by delirium, mania, delusions, and running amuck have been reported in India (Chopra and Chopra, 1942).

Musical Performance

The effect of marihuana on musical performance is particularly important because of the relative frequency of use among jazz musicians, who claim that it enhances their musical expression. Objective tests of musical performance and ability, however, fail to show any improvement. The impression of improved performance is partly attributable to the increased acuity of hearing and sensitivity to rhythm which occurs in the early phases of use. But even more important in this connection are the release of inhibition, which intensifies "the wild, emotional character of performance," and the depression of the self-critical faculty, which enhances "the subjective estimate of the individual's own performance (Walton, 1938).

Sex Activity

Much of the popular notoriety of marihuana is based on its so-called aphrodisiac properties. Some of the more sensational crimes committed under the influence of marihuana intoxication do indeed have a strong sexual coloration. Actually, however, there is no reliable evidence which points to any direct effect of the drug on sex drive. The lower spinal centers and the sex organs themselves are not affected.

> It is true that some individuals experience a marked stimulation of [sex] desires, but in a great proportion of other instances, no such

impulses are evident. The effect, again, is very probably due to removal of the usual restraints and correspondingly to the release of the more primitive impulses (Walton, 1938).

In any event, marihuana, unlike opiates, does not depress sex drives, except in some very long-standing cases.

The apparent erotic stimulation induced by marihuana in certain individuals, therefore, corresponds essentially to the release of inhibited personality trends. These persons, prior to drug use, tend to be excessively preoccupied with sexual gratification. Many also exhibit infantile and homosexual tendencies. In addition, the drug increases self-confidence and eliminates apprehension about the receptivity of the contemplated sex partner. Many users report that the sensual aspects of sexual enjoyment are prolonged as a consequence of the exaggerated perception of elapsed time. Exhibitions of perverted sexual practices ("circuses") are not an uncommon feature at "tea parties."

Crime

The relationship between marihuana use and the commission of violent crime is perhaps the most controversial issue relating to the drug. A fair summary of the available evidence would be that very rarely do major crimes follow upon use of the drug and that, in instances where they do, the relationship is an indirect one. In contrast to opiate addicts, habitual marihuana users tend to have preaddiction records of delinquency. Few, however, are professional criminals. Drunkenness, disorderly conduct, fighting, and petty thievery are the commonest offenses.

In most cases of violent crime associated with marihuana intoxication, the major determining factors are

> ... traits of character which lead to conflict with the law. Basically the urge for criminal activity must be present. Use of marihuana lessens or eliminates anxieties which interfere with the urge for lawlessness (Chopra and Chopra, 1933).

Thus it is clear that

> ... marihuana like alcohol does not necessarily produce abnormal behavior. The danger lies in the fact that immature and psychopathic persons use it to deaden their perception of reality, and when under its effects their inhibitions and judgment are impaired with consequent increase in abnormal behavior. . . . [It may act] as the determining

factor turning the balance in the direction of asocial behavior rather than permitting the poorly integrated social conscience of such an individual to remain in control (Gaskill, 1945).

In addition to releasing latent antisocial trends, marihuana may contribute to premeditated crime when used to bolster courage prior to involvement in planned delinquent activities. Some of the more sensational instances of homicide and sexual assault attributed to marihuana intoxication are undoubtedly manifestations of transitory psychotic states induced by the drug. Still another reason for the association of marihuana addiction and crime is the somewhat greater use of marihuana in slum-urban areas where delinquency rates tend to be high. Marihuana, by virtue of its stupefying effects, may sometimes inhibit the expression of aggressive impulses. In Vietnam, aggression and paranoid ideas were observed among heavy marihuana users (Mirkin and McKenna, 1975).

Permanent Psychological Effects

Exhaustive examination of chronic marihuana users in the United States has failed to yield any evidence of prolonged psychosis or mental deterioration (New York City Mayor's Committee on Marihuana, 1944). However, Chopra and Chopra reported that 3 percent of their clinical population in India exhibited signs of major psychological damage such as active psychosis (1933, 1942). The discrepancy between the American and Indian data can be explained perhaps by differences in the relative incidence and mean duration of chronic addiction and by differences in the preparations and dosage of the drug used in the two countries.

Conclusion

In conclusion, it can be stated that marihuana is a less effective analgesic and euphoria-producing drug than the opiates. Like alcohol it is more suitable for casual, recreational use and for a part-time escape from reality. It is more euphorogenous than alcohol, but its general psychological and behavioral properties—release of inhibitions, large individual differences in emotional response, impairment of intellectual functioning, motor incoordination, and idiosyncratic elicitation of aggressive tendencies—are very similar in nature.

Some of the recent American research (Robbins et al, 1970) has suggested a long-term "amotivational syndrome" among chronic marihuana users as compared to nonusers. The weight of the evidence, however (Beaubrun and Knight, 1973; Brill and Christie, 1974; Halikas et al., 1972; Hochman and Brill, 1973; Kolansky et al., 1972; National Commission on Marihuana and Drug Abuse, 1972) has failed to confirm this finding except in a minority (perhaps 10-12 percent) of long-term users. This issue is still unresolved and obviously requires further research. Thus, although caution is indicated in legalizing marihuana (Ausubel, 1970) it is clear that liberalization of the harsh and irrational marihuana penalities is long overdue.

Relation to Opiate Addiction

Prior to the 1950-1951 epidemic of marihuana use, it was generally believed (Charen and Perlman, 1946; Merrill, 1950) that "the use of marihuana [did] not lead to morphine or heroin or cocaine addiction, and no effort [was] made to create a market for these narcotics by stimulating the practice of marihuana smoking" (New York City Mayor's Committee on Marihuana, 1944). However, the typical sequence of drug use (from marihuana to heroin) during the teen-age outbreak of addiction in 1951 led to the belief that marihuana smoking per se increases the later likelihood of opiate addiction by creating an appetite for even bigger thrills (Bureau of Narcotics, U.S. Treasury Department).

As already pointed out, this sequence of events is not necessarily causal but is mostly a function of sociological concomitance under epidemic conditions. Reactive drug addicts exposed to both drugs, and having no personality preference for either, will obviously choose the most available, least expensive, and least dangerous one first. In the case of addicts with marked personality defects, however, there is unequivocal evidence of specificity of preference. Opiate addicts invariably prefer opiates and marihuana addicts prefer marihuana when free access to either drug prevails (Wikler, 1953; Charen and Perlman, 1946). Marihuana addicts (apart from the reactive variety) will only turn to opiates if their personality structure is such as to give the latter drugs preferential adjustive value. In such cases, marihuana use is not the determining factor in opiate addiction but at most a stepping-stone which lowers inner restraints. Marihuana addicts do use Benzedrine®, alcohol, nembutal, and nutmeg, but marihuana is the primary source of pleasure (Charen and Perlman, 1946).

Diagnosis, Prognosis, Treatment

Marihuana addiction is very difficult to recognize. "The outstanding finding is the odor which strongly resembles that of cubeb cigarettes. If this odor is detected and the patient's conjunctivae are markedly reddened, and garrulousness and hilarity are present, marihuana intoxication is quite likely" (Isbell, 1951). Differential diagnosis of the various kinds of marihuana addicts is extremely important and is based on the same procedures used for opiate addicts (see Chapter 3).

Prognosis and treatment are almost identical to that described for the analogous categories of opiate addiction except that there are no bothersome withdrawal symptoms. Habitual marihuana addicts show little desire for cure and tend to believe that the practice is neither harmful nor habit-forming. They tend to be irritable, garrulous, aggressive, and complaining.

Barbiturates

In recent years, addiction to the barbiturates has been growing at an alarming rate. The trend is a reflection of the generally high rate of postwar addiction and of the relatively easy availability of the drugs in comparison to opiates and marihuana. Opiate addicts frequently use barbiturates to tide them over periods when opiates are either unobtainable or in short supply. Like chronic alcoholics, barbiturate addicts may use the drug for a single night's debauch, for prolonged sprees, or daily for months or years. In many cases, barbiturates are used concomitantly with alcohol or amphetamines. Two indirect indices of the increased frequency of barbiturate addiction are the 1,000 percent increase in the manufacture of the drug since 1933 and the sharp rise in the number of accidental and suicidal deaths attributed to it.

Barbiturate addicts prefer the more potent, rapidly active drugs such as Nembutal® and Seconal®. The general argot term for barbiturates is *goof balls*. Special terms corresponding to color of the capsules *(yellow jackets, pink ladies)* are also in vogue. The customary dosage is 1.0 to 1.15 grams daily. They are usually taken orally, but some addicts prefer the intravenous route. Since they are extremely irritating they give rise to large abscesses if injected into the subcutaneous tissues. Most addicts obtain their drug supply by "working" several physicians simultaneously. Other sources are unethical pharmacists and dope peddlers. The Durham-Humphrey Act of 1951 made the sale of barbiturates without a prescription a federal offense. Many states and municipalities have also passed regulatory laws within the past five years.

Addiction Phenomena

In therapeutic doses barbiturates are among the most useful of all the sedatives and hypnotics. Larger doses, unlike opiates but like alcohol, result in ataxia, mental confusion, and emotional instability. For purposes of inducing either a borderline state of hypnosis in which resistance to psychiatric probing is reduced or a state of surgical anesthesia, sodium pentothal is administered intravenously.

Continued use of even therapeutic doses results in habituation or psychic dependence in the sense that patients experience difficulty in falling asleep or remaining emotionally composed when the drug is discontinued. This degree of physical and emotional dependence, however, is not serious and need not be viewed with alarm, if carefully supervised. Nevertheless, to minimize the possibility of serious addiction, the drug should be discontinued as quickly as possible and administered in as small and intermittent doses as are consistent with effectiveness. Prescriptions should be marked "not to be refilled," and physicians should ascertain whether patients are receiving the drug from several sources.

The serious barbiturate addict is not concerned with merely achieving sedation and relief of insomnia. As an inadequate personality or seriously agitated anxiety neurotic, he is desirous of the euphoria or separation from unpleasant realities that intoxicating doses of the drug can induce. Psychological habituation to this dosage is easily acquired in predisposed persons, and relapse frequently follows cure. The euphoria, however, cannot be experienced without the simultaneous occurrence of ataxia and mental confusion. Also, when as much as 0.8 grams is taken daily for two months or more, genuine physical dependence is invariably established, and discontinuance of the drug leads to an abstinence syndrome that is more severe and dangerous than in opiate addiction.

Symptoms of chronic barbiturate intoxication are also more disabling than is the case with opiate addiction. Thinking, judgment, reaction time, and general intellectual functioning are impaired. The addict is somnolent, confused, and emotionally unstable. Neurological symptoms include muscular incoordination, tremors, ataxia, nystagmus, dysarthria, and choreiform movements. Superficial reflexes may be absent. Patients typically

> offer shallow rationalizations for the obvious defects in their performance. . . . Frequently, they are obstinate, abusive and assaultive. . . . Masturbation is common and practiced openly by some. . . . Appetite is generally not impaired and often is enhanced (Wikler, 1953).

These latter symptoms are in marked contrast to those of opiate addiction. The diagnosis (when uncomplicated by alcoholism) "is suggested by signs resembling those of alcoholic intoxication but without any odor of alcohol on the breath" (Isbell, 1951).

Tolerance to barbiturates is limited, irregularly acquired, and somewhat idiosyncratic. The addict gradually increases his dosage, but the margin of tolerance is extremely narrow. For these reasons, it is doubtful whether genuine cellular tolerance is acquired or whether tolerance and physical dependence are related. Even though withdrawal signs are as invariable as in chronic alcoholism, it is more probable that they are reflective of *gross* disturbance of homeostatic equilibrium than of acquired cellular hypersensitivity.

After abrupt withdrawal of barbiturates, "the symptoms of intoxication abate and the patients appear to be improved" (Isbell, 1951). But within the first 24 hours they become apprehensive, restless, and weak. Tremors, hyperactive reflexes, insomnia, nausea, and vomiting may appear. Grand mal epileptiform seizures may or may not occur on the second or third day. In some cases, the convulsions are followed by a psychosis "which resembles alcoholic delirium tremens" (Isbell, 1951). It is characterized by disorientation, vivid hallucinations (usually visual), anxiety, and paranoid delusions. The delirium may be accompanied by fever, albuminuria, elevation of the N.P.N., and by elevated blood pressure, pulse, and respiratory rates. In untreated cases it may last for weeks, but the condition is self-limited "and patients recover completely, provided they are sufficiently protected and not allowed to become dangerously exhausted" (Isbell, 1951).

Treatment

Treatment should not be attempted in the patient's home or in a general hospital. He should first be stabilized on a dose of barbiturates sufficient to maintain mild intoxication. Although this will suppress convulsions it will not necessarily affect the course of the psychosis. Parenteral fluids, niacin, and other B-complex vitamins are usually indicated. Psychiatric and rehabilitative therapy are necessary but beyond the means of most patients. Barbiturate addicts were not admitted to the Public Health Service hospitals unless they were simultaneously addicted to opiates. In treating multiple (nonheroin) users of soft drugs, a "feedback" behavior modification program proved significantly more effective than a hospitalization program with regard to employment, work performance, and control of the drug problem (MacDonaugh, 1976).

Psychotropic Drugs

In recent years, such minor tranquilizers as Valium® and Librium®, antidepressants such as Elavil®, and hypnotics (e.g., Noludar®, Placidyl®, Doriden® and Quaalude®, have been subject to much abuse for euphoric purposes, particularly by patients in Methadone Maintenance Treatment Programs (see Valium® package insert, 1971; Placidyl® package insert, 1971). Intoxications and withdrawal syndromes similar to the barbiturates have been found for Valium®, Librium®, Doriden®, Placidyl®, and Quaalude®. In fact, a vast new army of addicts using these drugs has arisen in the late sixties and early seventies.

Despite much misinformed mass-media propaganda to the contrary, however, physical dependence seldom develops below a total daily dose of 30 mg. Eighty percent of minor tranquilizer prescriptions are written by the general practitioner, presumably to dispose of patients suspected of psychosomatic complaints or hypochondriasis, and to get them off the busy practitioner's back and out of his office. In the latter instance, these drugs help the physician evade his professional responsibility of ruling out nonpsychogenic, organic and functional disorders. Valium® and Librium®, in fact, are the most frequently prescribed drugs in the United States today.

Cocaine and the Amphetamines

In contrast to alcohol, marihuana, and the barbiturates which sometimes appear to be stimulants (because they release cortically-imposed inhibitions), cocaine and the amphetamines are genuine cortical stimulants. Cocaine is prepared from the leaf of the coca shrub.* It is a white, flaky-like substance called *snow* or *C* in addict's slang. Although largely replaced by procaine, it is still used as local anesthetic in eye surgery. Addicts usually take it intravenously, as much as two to three grams daily. It is also sniffed. Benzedrine® ("benny") is generally taken orally in tablet form (0.2 to 1.0 gram daily) by addicts.† Sometimes it is extracted from inhalers designed to counteract nasal congestion. Medically it is used as a cerebral stimulant and appetite depressant.

The Indian natives of the Andean regions of Peru, Bolivia, Argentina, Chile, Ecuador, and Colombia have been chewing the coca leaf ever since the Spanish conquest in 1537. The United Nations Narcotic Commission found in 1949 that 90 percent of the poverty-stricken Andean Indians chew coca leaves habitually to combat hunger, fatigue, and cold. In the United States, cocaine and the amphetamines are seldom used alone or taken continuously; the former drug is generally combined with heroin (as a "speed-ball"), and the latter with barbiturates to mitigate either extreme stimulant or depressant effects.

Both cocaine and Benzedrine® are used for their euphoric properties. They generate pleasurable feelings of elation and superiority, excitement, sleeplessness, and relief of fatigue. As their effects wear

---

* The commercial source of cocaine is Javanese coca. The South American coca leaves are a relatively poor source of the drug.
† Many amphetamine addicts take large doses of methadrene ("speed") intravenously. This practice leads to primary impairment of liver function. The effects of the drug are also greatly enhanced by this route of administration. Frantic, sleepless overactivity, often marked by paranoid ideas, is followed by virtual collapse. Many "speed" addicts also use large doses of barbiturates to counteract the hyperactivity and excitement of this condition and to taper off. Contrariwise, many barbiturate addicts use amphetamines for the opposite effects.

off, the addict feels weak, depressed, and restless. Sympathomimetic side effects include sweating, rapid heartbeat, elevated blood pressure, and pupillary dilatation. Undesired concomitant signs of cortical stimulation are nervousness, tremors, hyperactive tendon reflexes, and vivid hallucinations. The cocaine addict frequently imagines that insects are crawling on or under his skin and that miniature persons are swarming through the keyhole. Paranoid delusions, aggressive trends, and assaultiveness are not uncommon. "Hallucinations during Benzedrine® intoxication are similar to those of cocaine intoxication" (Isbell, 1951).

Although psychological habituation occurs in relation to both drugs, genuine tolerance is not developed and "there are no true withdrawal symptoms" (Isbell, 1951). Diagnosis in chronic cases is suggested by the unique combination of sympathomimetic symptoms, hyperactive tendon reflexes, hallucinations, delusions, loss of appetite, and emaciation. When cocaine is sniffed, the nasal septum may be ulcerated or perforated. Cocaine is specifically included in the Harrison Narcotic Act, and addicts were treated at the two narcotic hospitals maintained by the Public Health Service.

LSD and Other Hallucinogens

Subsequent to 1962, LSD, a drug originally used primarily for psychiatric and psychotherapeutic research, became popular with the youth drug culture to induce consciousness-expanding states. Synthesized on the black market, and used concomitantly with other similar drugs such as psilocybin, mescaline, and peyote, it was used by millions of young Americans. Its principal effects are hallucinations, mystical experience, perceptual enhancement, schizophreniclike and bizarre behavior, and suicidal attempts that sometimes last long after the drug is discontinued ("flashbacks"). Following the passage of restrictive legislation and the widespread publicity given to the not infrequent chromosomal damage and "bad trips" caused by the drug, the incidence of LSD use markedly declined. Now it is mostly used in research or experiments for psychotherapeutic purposes in alcoholism (Smart, et al., 1967) and other mental disorders.

Peyote and mescaline are primarily used by American Indians in the Southwest as part of various esoteric religious ceremonies. But in the sixties, they were also used by the same youth cultists who sought the psychedelic and hallucinogenic effects of LSD.

Phenclydine (PCP)

Since about 1967, two drugs have often been associated with marijuana use, i.e., phenclydine (PCP) commonly known as "angel dust" or "animal tranquilizer" and a toxic defoliant used to destroy marijuana plants in Mexico. In small doses it leads to such short-term effects as rapid and shallow breathing, increase in blood pressure and pulse rate, flushing, profuse perspiration, and numbness and incoordination of the extremities. Larger doses result in nausea, vomiting, blurred vision, loss of balance, dizziness, rolling and tearing of the eyes. Psychological effects mimic alcohol intoxication, schizophrenia (delusions, hallucinations), illusions, and mental confusion.

Solvents and Aerosols

Volatile hydrocarbons such as nitrous oxide ("laughing gas") have been used for over 100 years to induce euphoria. More recently, teen-agers have abused the fluorocarbons in aerosol sprays, carbon tetrachloride (stain remover), and model airplane glue or cement. Sometimes such use has led to fatal heart pathology and asphyxiation. More commonly, sniffing is accompanied by light-headedness, coma, muscular incoordination, and seizures.

Chapter 7
Prevention
of
Drug Addiction

In view of the discouraging prognosis of primary (adjustive) drug addiction, good prevention may be the best means of treatment (Committee on Public Relations of the New York Academy of Medicine, 1953, p. 17). Sober evaluation of the magnitude of the problem, however, leads to the realization that complete eradication of the evil is a commendable but probably unobtainable goal. Since immature and inadequate personalities will always be with us—even in a theoretically perfect society—it is reasonable to expect that some of them will somehow manage to procure and use narcotics illicitly. We can at best hope to hold the practice to a minimum. It is unrealistic to believe that even this goal could be realized within the very near future.

Because the causes of drug addiction are multiple, no *single* approach to prevention could possibly be successful. From a causative standpoint these three general approaches seem feasible:

(1) reducing the number of potential candidates for drug addiction;

(2) reducing the availability of narcotic drugs; and

(3) decreasing attitudinal tolerance toward the practice of drug addiction in a given community.

A fourth approach—research into the nature, causes, treatment, outcome, and epidemiology of drug addiction—can only be effective insofar as it has bearing on the factors of predisposition, availability, and attitudinal tolerance.

Reducing the Availability of Drugs

The most available and immediate approach to the reduction of the incidence of drug addiction . . . is to prevent individuals with motivationally immature personalities from gaining access to the drug. Although it is true that only a small proportion of persons exposed to opiates share this personality defect, it stands to reason that the larger number of individuals who are exposed, the larger will be the number of persons who develop true addiction (Ausubel, 1952a).

The [relative] paucity of morphine addicts today is not in any way due to a lack of potential candidates but to stringent government regulation governing morphine's sale, distribution, and prescription and to the relatively few persons knowingly exposed to morphine over long periods. The importance of the control factor in reducing opium addiction can be seen in the contrasting rise in barbiturate and amphetamine addiction because of lack of adequate safeguards in their distribution (Ausubel, 1948).

Law Enforcement

Reducing the availability of narcotics requires measures directed at all phases of the illicit traffic, from limitation of world production of opiates to legitimate needs and international regulation of distribution and use, on the one hand, to the prevention of smuggling and the destruction of organized, nationwide dope rings, on the other. For these purposes, both the United States Commission on Narcotics and the Drug Enforcement Administration require greater authority and appropriations. More effective and honest law enforcement is required at the state and municipal levels to apprehend and convict powerful racketeers with political influence and to prevent the diversion of opiates from legitimate stocks.

The alert physician can cooperate in this aspect of prevention by limiting the use of opiates to their indispensable indications; by keeping the dosage as small, infrequent, and intermittent as possible; by discontinuing their use at the earliest possible moment; by refraining from informing the patient that he is receiving the drug; and by using salicylates or codeine in chronic, less painful conditions. Physicians must also learn to recognize drug addicts, to resist their clever schemes and importunities, and to avoid administering opiates for alcoholic debauches or neurotic symptoms. Precautions in the prescription of barbiturates have already been discussed.

Legislation

With respect to needed legislation, the two most important measures are subsititution of mandatory hospital treatment, as well as outpatient treatment, for the present criminal status of addiction (illegal possession of narcotics) in the case of addict peddlers, and imposition of stiffer penalities on nonaddict peddlers. It has been demonstrated that the rate of addiction in a given state is directly proportional to the severity of its laws regarding narcotic violations. Addict peddlers should not be immune to punishment. However, it is morally less reprehensible to sell narcotics merely to support one's own habit than to traffic wholesale in human misery for financial gain. Also, for purposes of apprehending and convicting the bigtime peddlers, it is necessary to obtain the small pusher's cooperation by dealing leniently with him. The Boggs Law and the "Rockefeller" laws in New York State fail to differentiate between these two kinds of narcotics violators.

Within the past five years the federal government and many states have enacted other desirable legislation restricting the spread or hazards of drug addiction. The sale of barbiturates and of hypodermic needles and syringes is being regulated more carefully. Laws have been passed reducing the amount of narcotic drugs necessary to be found on the person of a defendant before he can be charged with felonious possession, permitting the seizure and forfeiture of vehicles used in narcotics traffic, making forgery of prescriptions more difficult, and prohibiting addicts from driving automobiles or possessing firearms.

Reducing Attitudinal Tolerance

Since attitudinal tolerance in the immediate cultural milieu is such an important selective factor in determining the occurrence of drug addiction, measures aimed at lowering this tolerance are an important aspect of any preventive program. The eradication of the drug evil in a community where it takes root requires coordinated and sustained mobilization of public opinion and effective remedial action based on actual assessment of the local situation. At the same time, city-wide programs can be organized and integrated by an official, central body responsible to the mayor and empowered to implement the conclusions it reaches. In any event, however, the principles of local initiative and autonomy, and of the utilization of resident talent and resources, demonstrated so forcefully by the Chicago Area Projects in relation to juvenile delinquency, should not be ignored. No program of community betterment can be superimposed from above and retain vitality and genuine citizen participation for any length of time.

The problem of drug addiction cannot, of course, be separated from the wider problems of substandard housing, malnutrition, disease, poverty, and racial and ethnic discrimination which coexist with it in slum-urban areas. Elimination of these conditions and the provision of wholesome substitutes for antisocial gang activities would go a long way toward removing the factors that enhance availability of drugs, social tolerance toward drug use, and individual predispositions toward reactive utilization of drugs. Such measures, however, are no panacea, as can be readily appreciated when one considers that the addict population is drawn from all strata of society and that most slum-dwelling adolescents do not become even transitory addicts.

Adult Instruction

Adult, parent, and teacher education is obviously part of any program aimed at reducing social tolerance for the drug habit. But again it serves little purpose if drug addiction is not an actual or potential problem in a given community. Public lectures, symposia, newspaper and magazine articles, and films can do much to create a proper climate of public opinion if they are informed, accurate, and factual. Unfortunately, much of the existing educational material is lurid, inaccurate, and oversimplified.

Lastly, it should be mentioned that insofar as addiction is a communicable disease which is spread in part by the personal influence of addicts on potential addicts, the treatment and cure of prognostically hopeful cases and the segregation of incorrigible cases can eliminate important sources of contagion.

School Instruction

Laws in practically all of the states and territories of the United States require that the public schools provide instruction for children about the nature and effects of narcotic drugs. But because most teachers are inadequately informed about this subject, these laws are frequently disregarded or at best poorly and halfheartedly implemented. This is truly unfortunate, for although education is certainly no panacea for the prevention of drug addiction, the school is the best equipped and most strategically located institution for undertaking preventive instruction.

A realistically oriented instructional program in the schools would seek to accomplish the following three major objectives (Ausubel and Spalding, 1956):

1. *Engender beliefs and attitudes that drug addiction is harmful to the best interests of both the individual and society.* The argument that persons predisposed to drug addiction would not be affected by education, and that those who are not so predisposed do not need it, only holds true for individuals with extreme predispositions in either direction. Preliminary evidence of the effects of narcotics education in a New York City school indicate that pupils who received intensive instruction—"even those who were admitted users—displayed a sense of revulsion and individual resolution and awareness of the awful consequences with respect to drugs which were not nearly so evident in the statements made" by pupils in another school who did not receive instruction (New York City Board of Education, 1951).

2. *Reduce the tendency to experiment with narcotic drugs that proceeds from curiosity, ignorance, and from peer group and adult pressures.* Part of this aspect of the program is to "fortify youth with protective devices against the approaches . . . insinuation . . . and threats" they are likely to encounter (C. C. Baldwin, Committee on Public Relations, New York Academy of Medicine, 1951). The objective here is not to terrify children with exaggerated, lurid, and only half-true forebodings of disaster if they use narcotic drugs, since such fear campaigns seldom function effectively as deterrents. We do believe, however, that frank, honest, and open discussion weakens the temptation toward surreptitious experimentation and

that an attitude of secrecy and avoidance does just the opposite. This is especially true during adolescence when boys and girls seem particularly eager to flaunt adult-imposed norms and standards that are regarded as too sacrosanct even to discuss.

3. *Acquaint pupils with authentic evidence concerning the nature and effects of narcotic drugs and with related social and economic problems.* This information should constitute part of any adult's general education.

It would be extremely naive to suppose that there are no hazards involved in instructing children about narcotic drugs in the public schools. The most patent danger is the possibility of misinformed and incompetent instruction by teachers who are unacquainted with both recent scientific evidence and the sociological facts of life in this area. The unfortunate consequences of this kind of instruction are most striking and immediate where the information provided by teachers finds ready contradiction in the daily personal experience of children. For example, in the slum areas of New York and Chicago, pupils are apt to know a great deal about narcotic drugs and can easily detect untrue or overgeneralized statements. This unfortunate situation, however, is in large part preventable if suitable teacher training and in-service programs are available.

A second kind of hazard frequently mentioned is somewhat more controversial and, depending on one's point of view, may be considered either irremediable or largely specious. Many experienced observers, for example, the former Director of the Federal Bureau of Narcotics, and experts serving on the United Nations Commission on Narcotic Drugs, are strongly opposed to narcotics education on the grounds that it stimulates curiosity and encourages young people to experiment with drugs (Meyer, 1952). On the other hand, equally competent authorities point out that

> . . . we do not avoid marking a thin spot on the ice of a skating pond because we fear some daredevil may be lured to try it. Nor do we avoid teaching a small child the dangers of fire because he may become an arsonist. If we are unable in our schools to make a case against drug addiction, then we are either ignorant of its awful consequences or we should admit nothing can be taught (C. C. Baldwin, Committee on Public Relations, New York Academy of Medicine, 1951).

In our opinion, this latter position makes more educational sense than the former. The value of an ostrichlike approach to social problems has never been demonstrated. Sound educational methods that avoid both glamorization of dangerous practices and preoccupation with unnecessary pictorial details tend to reduce rather than to stimulate the impulse toward experimentation. In the case of children who are already or potentially exposed to drug addiction, the question of *arousing* curiosity is irrelevant; the problem is to counteract *existing* curiosity. In the case of children living in rural or suburban neighborhoods who are unlikely to be exposed, curiosity, if aroused, can cause little harm since drugs are not generally accessible in such areas (C. C. Baldwin, Committee on Public Relations, New York Academy of Medicine, 1953). In any event, no cases of drug addiction directly attributable to the influence of school instruction have been reported in New York City (J. Toolan, Committee on Public Relations, New York Academy of Medicine, 1953).

It is self-evident that the type of educational program about narcotics that is offered in a given school must take into account the actual or potential extent of the drug-addiction problem in the community. In a slum-urban area, for example, it would be quite appropriate to familiarize children with the approaches used by drug peddlers. In a rural school, on the other hand, such instruction would be completely indefensible.

The preparation of a unit on narcotic drugs should not present any special difficulties to a resourceful and well-trained teacher. This material can be most effectively taught when appropriately incorporated into existing subject-matter fields. The creation of special courses of study on narcotic drugs focuses undue attention on this subject and throws it out of proper perspective.

The teacher should be cautioned against the discussion of individual cases or bizarre occurrences brought up by pupils. Such information is often inaccurate and based on hearsay. Emphasis should be placed on factual material and on general principles. If case histories are used for illustrative purposes, their authenticity should be verified. In communities where drug addiction is endemic, it is important for teachers to know the more commonly used terms of the addicts's argot.*

Apart from classroom instruction, teachers can help in identifying and referring for guidance children who use narcotics, and in cooperating with parents, law-enforcement bodies, and social agencies concerned with narcotics control.

Finally, it should be remembered that the school is one of the important character- and personality-building institutions in our society. To the extent that teachers help children become mature, responsible, and well-integrated individuals; to the extent that schools help in providing wholesome status-giving and recreational activities for adolescent boys and girls; to the extent that channels of communication between pupils and teachers are kept open in a friendly and democratic atmosphere; and to the extent that maladjusted pupils are identified early in their school careers and provided with competent guidance, the problems of drug addiction will in large measure be aborted before drugs ever gain a dangerous foothold in the communities of our nation.

Reducing the Number of Potential Addicts

The long-range preventive approach to drug addiction involves an attempt to influence personality development in home, school, and play group in ways that reduce the incidence of those personality predispositions favoring the occurrence of addiction. The extension of parent education and parent guidance in child rearing may help decrease the incidence of overprotective, overpermissive, and overdominating practices. Another possibility is to identify and provide long-term guidance of motivationally immature children and adolescents. Provisions for early identification and follow-up treatment of adolescents in the initial and experimental phases of addiction might logically be considered part of this aspect of prevention. The Regional Medical Counseling Clinics established by the Sixty-seventh Illinois General Assembly were partly intended to serve this function.

---

* See D.W. Maurer. Argot of the underworld narcotic addicts. *American Speech*, October 1938; M. Mezzrow and B. Wolfe. *Really the Blues*, New York: Random House, 1946; and E. Partridge. *Dictionary of Slang and Unconventional English*, 3rd Ed., London: Routledge and Kegan Paul, 1949.

Research

Before proposing some future directions for psychiatric research in drug addiction among adolescents, it might be helpful first to take a critical backward glance and review some of the shortcomings of past research efforts. Why has our knowledge about the nature, causes, and prevention of drug addiction grown so slowly over the past three decades (Ausubel, 1966)?

The Pharmacological Approach

In the first place, we have focused too large a share of our past research energies on the chemical, pharmacological, neurophysiological, and psychopharmacological aspects of addiction, and have been insufficiently concerned both with the psychological factors that predispose a person toward addiction, and with the sociological factors that convert this predisposition into a behavioral and clinical entity. We have no quarrel with the wholly laudable aim of extending our knowledge about the sites and mechanisms of action of the various narcotic drugs, of discovering how these drugs produce their behavioral effects, and of relating pharmacological actions to chemical structure. But such knowledge, valuable as it is, can at most explain how particular drugs affect our bodies, emotions, and behavior, and, hence, define their potential adjustive properties. It cannot explain why these potential adjustive characteristics of drugs are adjustive, in fact, for some persons but not for others. It cannot, in other words, account for the selective incidence of drug addiction.

It also appears that we have been overimpressed in the past with the possibility of preventing drug addiction by chemically dissociating those features of narcotic drugs responsible for relief from pain, and those features responsible for undesirable side effects and addiction phenomena. At first the aim was to synthesize a potent analgesic that did not simultaneously produce withdrawal symptoms. This goal was partly achieved by German chemists prior to World War II with the discovery of methadone; but since withdrawal symptoms play only a minor role in the causation of drug addiction, and seldom, if ever, deter true addicts from using drugs, methadone proved to be no more and no less addicting than other narcotics. Chemists and pharmacologists then directed their efforts toward removing the euphorogenous effects of narcotic drugs. Theoretically, of course, this is no easy task since the pain-reducing properties of a drug are largely dependent upon its ability to produce euphoria. Nevertheless, even if this attempt should prove entirely successful*, would it really help much in eradicating our drug addiction problem? True, fewer addicts would be introduced to drugs through the medium of medical therapy; but epidemiologically speaking, this is a relatively minor route of introduction. Both heroin and marihuana have long since been removed from the *Pharmacopoea,* but addicts are not known for their fastidiousness in consulting the *Pharmacopoea* before using a drug.

Single Versus Multiple Causality

A second difficulty with previous research efforts has been a tendency to conceptualize the drug addiction problem in terms of single causality. Etiological thinking about drug addiction has been hampered by the same conceptual error that has plagued the investigation of the causes of such other complex disorders as cancer and juvenile delinquency. This is the error of assuming that since the disorder in question is overtly similar in all individuals, it must necessarily have the same single cause in all instances. Thus, psychiatrists and clinical psychologists tend to be preoccupied with the psychological characteristics of various drugs which have differential adjustive properties for different personality configurations; whereas social psychologists and sociologists tend to concentrate on differential attitudinal tolerance toward drugs prevailing in different communities and on socially-conditioned values, aspirations and motivations influencing addiction-proneness. Actually, of course, since the causes of drug addiction are multiple and additive in their impact, idiosyncratic and socially-conditioned personality factors are in no sense mutually exclusive. And even from the standpoint of the clinician, addiction to narcotics is hardly a unitary disorder. The anxiety neurotic who uses opiates for their sedative value has a much different malady than the motivationally inadequate personality who uses them to obtain immediate and effortless hedonistic

---

* See Chapter 2.

satisfaction and to dull his self-critical faculty; and both of these persons differ greatly from the aggressive but essentially normal adolescent growing up in an urban slum tolerant to addiction who uses drugs in order to identify with a certain type of deviant peer culture and as a nonspecific means of revolting against the norms of conventional society.

Methodological Difficulties
in Clinical Research

Turning now to some past shortcomings in clinical research methods, we may use the work at the United States Public Health Service Hospital in Lexington, Kentucky, as typical of much of the research in this field. Undoubtedly, much valuable clinical research has been conducted at the Lexington hospital. This hospital had the research advantages of a large population and variety of drug addicts who could be studied continuously over extended periods of time in a controlled environment. Other important advantages included the possibility of experimental addiction and the availability of scientists in many different fields for interdisciplinary study. Nevertheless, the clinical research at Lexington, although pointing to the existence of deep-rooted personality disturbances in drug addicts, lacks definitiveness for a number of methodological reasons.

First, with the exception of a few pioneering studies on small and unrepresentative samples of juvenile drug users, this research has neglected the highly significant consideration of a control group. The importance of a control group inheres in the fact that most Lexington addicts have been diagnosed as motivationally immature personalities or inadequate personalities. But most of them were also products of a lower-class, slum-urban, minority-group subculture characterized by low achievement motivation, little long-range planning, rebellious attitudes toward authority and conventional values, and preoccupation with immediate hedonistic gratification, kicks, and thrills. The problem thus arose to what extent the personality structure of addict patients was reflective of idiosyncratic temperamental and developmental factors, and to what extent it was simply reflective of the values of lower-class "cat" culture. Only by using matched groups of control (i.e., nonaddict) subjects from the same cultural environment was it possible for

Ausubel (1947), Gerard and Kornetsky (1955), and Chein and associates (1964) to demonstrate that juvenile addicts manifested significantly more personality pathology, adjustive difficulties, pathogenic family background, and disturbed parent-child relationships than could be expected from adolescents growing up in this particular subculture.

Second, most of the clinical studies at Lexington and Bellevue hospitals have been conducted on older groups of confirmed addicts who had been members of both the addict and criminal subcultures for many years. Hence, it was easy to confound predisposing preaddiction personality factors with postaddiction personality traits reflective of chronic addiction experience and criminal activities and associations. This difficulty, however, has been largely resolved by the more recent study of juvenile addicts.

A third methodological problem arose from the fact that the psychological responses of withdrawn addicts in a hospital setting could not be assumed to be identical with those of drug users in their typical social environment. Related problems stemmed from the examining psychiatrist's knowledge of who is and who is not an addict, his tendency to assume in advance that addicts are psychologically abnormal, and his unfamiliarity with the attitudinal and motivational norms of lower-class groups.

Last, there is the serious research problem of obtaining a representative sample of drug users (Ausubel, 1966; Sutker and Alain, 1973). The clinical populations of addicts that have been studied to date have not been representative of the total population of drug users. Recruited from Lexington, Bellevue, and Riverside hospitals, etc., for the most part, they constituted the more seriously disturbed and prognostically least hopeful of the addict population. Furthermore, we know now that the majority of juvenile drug users are casual, weekend "joy-poppers" who never become physiologically dependent, and that although delinquent gangs tend to condone experimentation with drugs, they strongly disapprove of and penalize habitual users. Preliminary evidence from the Research Center for Human Relations (1957) also suggests that ecological factors largely account for juvenile experimentation with narcotics, whereas personality factors account for chronic habituation (addiction).

To profit, therefore, from previous methodological inadequacies in clinical research on drug addiction, we must work with newly addicted young addicts, use a large and representative sample of drug addicts in our clinical population, and study released addicts in outpatient clinics and in their indigenous social environment as well as in closed-ward hospitals. In addition, it is important to use a matched control group drawn from the same sociocultural environment, and to shield the identity of the addict and control subjects from the examining psychiatrist and clinical psychologist when they make their personality assessments. Lastly, genuine addicts and mere users should not be part of the same research population, but should be studied as separately constituted groups.

Needed Clinical and Social Research

What are some of the more pressing clinical problems demanding further research? First, we need more intensive, controlled, and longitudinal study of the differential personality makeup and development of the casual drug user, on the one hand, and the more serious, habitual drug user or addict, on the other. What are the respective parent-child and age-mate relationships of these two groups like? How do the two groups differ in these respects during early adolescent development? When are the differences between the two groups first noticeable? When do the differences definitely crystallize?

The problem of differential diagnosis is made more difficult by the fact that the motivationally immature type of addict is found most commonly (although by no means as exclusively as is the casual drug user) among adolescent and young adult males in urban slum areas. This is hardly surprising when one considers that motivational immaturity is no more rare in such areas than elsewhere, and that the actual development of addiction in these highly susceptible individuals is further abetted by adolescent stresses, gang influences, racial and social class tensions, social demoralization, high availability of narcotics, and high community tolerance for the drug habit.

Second, we need more intensive differential study of the personality characteristics of the two principal types of long-term, habitual drug users—the inadequate psychopath with a motivationally immature hedonistic personality who shoots the drug "mainline" for its euphoric effects, and the motivationally mature neurotic who uses small, stabilized doses of narcotics for their sedative effects. Does the neurotic drug addict mainly suffer from anxiety? My own research at Lexington (1947) showed that a typical group of inadequate personality addicts was overwhelmingly more free of anxiety than was a group of normal controls.

Third, is there really such a clinical entity as medical addiction, that is, individuals with essentially normal personalities who become accidentally addicted during the course of illness, and then experience difficulty in breaking their physical dependence on narcotics? If so, what is the cause of their difficulty in overcoming physical dependence? Could it be that their tolerance for pain or discomfort is relatively low in comparison with that of normal persons or other kinds of addicts?

Fourth, we need to know more about the specificity of drug preference among addicts. Is there a characteristic personality syndrome for each kind of drug preference such as alcohol, marihuana, barbiturates, cocaine, and the opiates? Existing clinical study of this problem has been superficial to date. The contrasting psychopharmacological properties of marihuana and heroin, for example, allow for casual recreational use of the drug, on the one hand, and for a more complete and full-time escape from reality, on the other, for an accentuation of visceral satisfactions, in one instance, and for an obliteration of the appetitive drives, in the other.

Fifth, what are some of the important personality and social background factors that affect prognosis, the outcome of therapy, and the possibility of relapse? Our knowledge of these problems is sparse indeed.

Sixth, exactly how do community tolerance, conformity pressures in the peer group, and other ecological variables operate at each stage in the addiction process and in the occurrence of relapse? The Research Center for Human Relations (1957) has shed some light on these issues, but much more is needed.

Lastly, what about the value of different forms of therapy in drug addiction? How efficacious are individual psychotherapy, group psychotherapy, and vocational rehabilitation in terms of length of abstinence from drugs? Are different kinds of therapy indicated in different types of addiction? The good work records of many addicts during World War II, the satisfactory institutional adjustment achieved by many addicts, and the hopeful prognostic significance of possessing a marketable trade, all point to the great potential value of vocational rehabilitation. Nevertheless, none of the major treatment institutions has ever given this therapeutic possibility a really satisfactory trial.

In conclusion, we cannot realistically look forward to any dramatic breakthroughs in clinical drug addiction research. Progress will come only from the gradual accumulation of painstaking research findings. We need the same kind of systematic and intensive research effort dealing with the psychological and ecological aspects of addiction, and the same kind of methodological rigor and sophistication that has been exhibited in studying the chemical, pharmacological, and physiological aspects of the problem. Existing treatment centers, however, do not have the necessary staff to carry on this type of research. Without long-term programs sponsored by some federal agency such as the National Institute of Mental Health or by university centers of psychosociological research, such as the Research Center for Human Relations at New York University, it is unlikely that we will make much progress in realizing these research objectives.

Glossary*

Abstinence syndrome—a constellation of symptoms induced by abrupt withdrawal of opiates or barbiturates in addicted persons. Synonymous with *withdrawal syndrome.*

Addiction—habituation to the effects of a drug that is sufficiently extreme to result in disruption of normal bodily functioning and the appearance of mental and physical symptoms if the drug is suddenly discontinued.

Agenesis—lack of development.

Albuminuria—the presence of albumin in the urine; occurs sometimes in the barbiturate abstinence syndrome.

Alkaloid—the basic organic active compound(s) found in drugs derived from plants that are responsible for their pharmacological effects.

Analgesia—a state of diminished sensitivity to painful stimuli.

Anorexia—a state of diminished appetite for food; a characteristic symptom of opiate addiction.

Aphrodisiac—a drug which stimulates or enhances sexual desire.

Ataxia—gross muscular incoordination; sometimes found in the barbiturate and Valium® abstinence syndromes.

Barbiturate—a class of drugs derived from barbituric acid which act as sedatives and hypnotics, and sometimes as analgesics. See *sedative, hypnotic,* and *analgesic.*

Choreiform movements—irregular, jerky movements; sometimes found in the barbiturate abstinence syndrome.

Diuretic—a drug which increases the production of urine.

Dysarthria—impaired articulation of speech due to structural or functional disorders of the nervous system; sometimes found in the barbiturate abstinence syndrome.

Etiological—causal.

Euphoria—an ecstatic state of well-being and contentment not warranted by an individual's actual circumstances; induced by opiates, marihuana, cocaine, and large doses of barbiturates, amphetamines, Valium® and Elavil®, etc.

Grand mal seizures—attacks of tonic and/or clonic convulsions and loss of consciousness typical of grand mal epilepsy; also found in the barbiturate abstinence syndrome.

---

* Only includes medical and other technical or jargon terms used in this work. Terms defined in the text itself are not included unless they are used before they are formally defined.

Hallucinogen—a drug that typically or sometimes causes hallucinations (e.g., LSD, marihuana).

Hedonistic—pleasure-seeking or motivated by the desire for pleasure.

Heroin (diacetylmorphine)—a semisynthetic derivative of morphine used by opiate addicts. Its manufacture in or importation into the United States is forbidden by law.

Hyperactivity—overactivity.

Hypnotic—a drug that induces sleep; includes all narcotics, but refers more specifically to drugs the main action of which is to induce normal sleep.

Intractable—severe condition (e.g., pain) that is unresponsive to treatment (e.g., opiates).

"Joy-pops"—addict jargon for subcutaneous injections of an opiate, typically in a beginning user who is not yet physically dependent on the drug.

Lacrimation—secretion of tears. Excessive lacrimation is typical of the opiate abstinence syndrome.

Mainline—addict jargon for the intravenous route of injection.

Narcotic—a class of drugs which induce sleep and stupor and relieve pain; includes opiates, barbiturates, anesthetics, and others.

NPN—the nonprotein nitrogens of the blood.

Nystagmus—involuntary, rapid movement of the eyeball.

Opiate—a class of drugs which have the properties and actions of opium; includes opium itself and derivatives of opium, as well as synthetic opiatelike drugs not derived from opium (e.g. Demerol®, methadone).

Physical (or physiological) dependence—an altered bodily state developed by opiate, alcohol, tranquilizer, and barbiturate addicts; manifested externally by the appearance of a stereotyped pattern of symptoms (abstinence syndrome) upon abrupt withdrawal of the drug. See *tolerance.*

Psychotropic drugs—drugs altering mood or behavior. Therapeutically they include chiefly tranquilizers, antidepressants and antipsychotics.

Sedative—a drug that reduces activity and allays excitement.

Sympathomimetic drug—a drug which produces effects similar to those following stimulation of sympathetic nerve fibers (for example, epinephrine, amphetamines), i.e., rapid heartbeat, elevated blood pressure.

Tachycardia—excessively rapid heartbeat; a symptom of the opiate abstinence syndrome.

Thrombophlebitis—an inflammatory condition of a vein accompanied by clots blocking the flow of blood; a common condition in addicts who take opiates intravenously.

Tolerance—a state of increased bodily resistance to the actions of a drug acquired by an addicted person, enabling him to endure without harm doses that would have toxic or lethal effects on nonaddicted persons.

Tranquilizer—a class of drugs that reduce anxiety (e.g., Valium®, Librium®, Vistaril®).

Withdrawal syndrome—see *abstinence syndrome.*

References

Opiate Addiction

Amsel, Z., W. Mandel, L. Matthias, C. Mason, and I. Hocherman. Reliability and validity of self-reported illegal activities and drug use collected from narcotic addicts. *The International Journal of the Addictions,* 1976, *11,* 325-36.

Andrews, H. L. Biophysical studies of drug addiction. *Hospital News,* 1941, *8,* 14-18.

Anslinger, H. J., and W. F. Tompkins. *The Traffic in Narcotics.* New York: Funk & Wagnalls, 1953.

Aron, W. S., and D. W. Dailey. Graduates and splitees from therapeutic community drug treatment programs. *The International Journal of the Addictions,* 1976, *11,* 1-18.

Ausubel, D. P. Personality predispositions in drug addiction: a study of 80 matched addicts and controls. Unpublished manuscript, U.S. Public Health Service Hospital, Lexington, Ky., 1947.

Ausubel, D. P. The psychopathology and treatment of drug addiction in relation to the mental hygiene movement. *Psychiatric Quarterly, Supp.,* part 2, 1948, *22,* 219-50.

Ausubel, D. P. An evaluation of recent adolescent drug addiction. *Mental Hygiene,* 1952, *36,* 373-82.(a)

Ausubel, D. P. *Ego Development and the Personality Disorders.* New York: Grune & Stratton, 1952.(b)

Ausubel, D. P. Controversial issues in the management of drug addiction: legalization, ambulatory treatment and the British System. *Mental Hygiene,* 1960, *44,* 535-44.

Ausubel, D. P. Causes and types of drug addiction: a psychosocial view. *Psychiatric Quarterly,* 1961, *35,* 523-31.

Ausubel, D. P. The case for compulsory closed ward treatment of narcotic addicts. In *Medical Views on the Narcotics Problem:* Annual Judicial Conference of the Second Judicial Circuit of the United States. *Federal Rules Decisions,* 1962, 53-59.

Ausubel, D. P. The Dole-Nyswander treatment of heroin addiction. *Journal of the American Medical Association,* March 14, 1966, *195,* 949-50.(a)

Ausubel, D. P. Some future directions for research in adolescent drug addiction. *Adolescence,* 1966, *1,* 70-78.(b)

Ausubel, D. P., and Pearl Ausubel. Research on ego development among segregated Negro children. In *Education in Depressed Areas* (A. H. Passow, ed.). New York: Teachers College, Columbia University, 1963, pp. 109-41.

Ausubel, D. P., B. B. Karsten, and Laura Ausubel. Psychiatric disorders in treated narcotic addicts as a function of social class, race, and ethnicity. *The International Journals of the Addictions,* 1978, in press.

Ausubel, D. P., and W. B. Spalding. *Alcohol and narcotic drugs: a teachers' manual.* Springfield, Ill. Office of Superintendent of Public Instruction, 1956.

Battegay, R., D. Ladewig, R. Mühlemann, and N. Weidman. The culture of youth and drug abuse in some European countries. *The International Journal of the Addictions,* 1976, *11,* 245-62.

Berst, R. H. New hope for drug addicts. *Look,* November 30, 1965, 23-27.

Blumberg, H. H., S. D. Cohen, B. Elizabeth Dronfield, Elizabeth A. Mordecai, J. C. Roberts, and D. Hawks. Opiate use in London. *The Journal of the American Medical Association,* 1975, *232,* 131-32.

Brecher, E. M. and the Editors of Consumers Union. *Licit and Illicit Drugs.* Mt. Vernon, N. Y.: Consumers Union, 1972.

Brown, B. S., S. K. Gauvey, M. B. Meyers, and S. D. Stark. In their own words . . . addicts' reasons for initiating and withdrawing from heroin. *The International Journal of the Addictions,* 1971, *6,* 635-45.

Brown, B. S., D. R. Jansen, and Gloria J. Benn. Changes in attitude toward methadone. *Archives of General Psychiatry,* 1975, 32.

Bureau of Narcotics, U.S. Treasury Department. *Traffic in opium and dangerous drugs.* Washington, D.C.: U.S. Government Printing Office, Annual Reports.

Cabinet Interdepartmental Committee on Narcotics. *Report to the President,* February 1, 1956.

Cantanzaro, R. J. Alcohol and other drug dependencies: Ten basic concepts. *Journal of the Florida Medical Association,* 1971, *58,* 47-51.

Chappel, J. N., E. C. Senay, and J. J. Jaffe. Cyclazocine in a multimodality treatment program: comparative results. *International Journal of the Addictions,* 1971, *6,* 509-23.

Chein, I., *et al. The Road to H.* New York: Basic Books, 1964.

Cohen, M., A. Howard, D. F. Klein, and K. Newfield. Evaluating outcome criteria used in methadone maintenance programs. *The International Journal of the Addictions,* 1976, *11,* 283-94.

Collier, W. V., and Y. A. Hijazi. A follow-up study of former residents of a therapeutic community. *International Journal of the Addictions,* 1974, *9,* 804-26.

Committee on Public Health Relations of the New York Academy of Medicine. *Conference on Drug Addiction Among Adolescents.* New York: Blakiston, 1953.

Covi, L., R. S. Lippman, J. H. Pattison, et al. Length of treatment with anxiolytic sedatives and responses to their sudden withdrawal. *Acta Psychiatric Scandinavia,* 1973, *49,* 57-64.

Dai, B. *Opium Addiction in Chicago.* Shanghai, China: Commercial Press, 1937.

De Long, J. V. The methadone habit. *New York Times Magazine,* March 16, 1975.

Dole, V. P., and Marie E. Nyswander. A medical treatment of Diacetyl-morphine (heroin). *Journal of the American Medical Association,* August 23, 1965, *195,* 646-50.

Dole, V. P., and Marie E. Nyswander. Addiction—a metabolic disease. *Archives of International Medicine,* 1967, *120,* 19-24.

Eisenlohr, L. E. S. *International Narcotics Control.* London: Allen & Unwin, 1935.

Finestone, H. Narcotics and criminality. *Law and Contemporary Problems,* 1955, *22,* 69-85.

Gearing, Frances R. Successes and failures in methadone maintenance treatment of heroin addicts in New York City. *Proceedings, Third Methadone Conference,* New York, 1970.

Gerard, D. L., and C. Kornetsky. Adolescent opiate addiction: a study of control and addict subjects. *Psychiatric Quarterly,* 1955, *29,* 457.

Goldstein, N. L. *Narcotics, 1952.* Albany, N.Y.: Department of Law, 1953.

Goodman, L. S. and A. Gilman (eds.) *The Pharmacological Basis of Therapeutics* (4th edition), 1970.

Gritz, Ellen R., et al. Physiological and psychological effects of methadone in man. *Archives of General Psychiatry,* 1975, *32,* 237-42.

Hentoff, N. The treatment of addicts. *New Yorker,* June 26, 1965, 32-37; July 3, 1965, 32-57.

Her Majesty's Government in the United Kingdom of Great Britain and Northern Ireland. *Report to the United Nations on the working of international treaties on narcotic drugs for 1954.*

Hill, H. E., C. E. Haertzen, and H. Davis. An MMPI factor analytic study of alcoholics, narcotic addicts and criminals. *Quarterly Journal for the Study of Alcoholism,* 1962, *23,* 411.

Horrock, N. M. Drug agency has failed to stop drugs. *New York Times,* Sunday, May 25, 1974, section 4, page 3.

Illinois Department of Public Health. Springfield, Ill.: *Medical counselling clinics for narcotic addicts,* 1953.

Isbell, H. *What to Know about Drug Addiction.* Public Health Service Publication No. 94. Washington, D.C.: U.S. Government Printing Office, 1951.

Jaffe, J. J. Narcotic analgesics. Drug addiction and drug abuse. In *The Pharmacological Basis of Therapeutics* (L. S. Goodman and A. Gilman, eds.). New York: Macmillan, 1970, pp. 237-75; 276-313.

Joint Committee of the American Bar Association and the American Medical Association on Narcotic Drugs. *Interim Report*, 1958.

Khantzian, D. J., J. E. Mack, and A. F. Schatzberg. Heroin use as an attempt to cope: clinical observations. *American Journal of Psychiatry*, 1974, *131*, 160-64.

Kline, N. S., Choh Hao Li, H. E. Ledmann, A. Lajtha, E. Laski, and T. Cooper. B-Endorphic induced changes in schizophrenic and depressed patients. *Archives of General Psychology*, 1977, *34:* 1111-13.

Klinge, V., H. Vaziri and K. Lennox. Comparison of psychiatric inpatient male and female drug abusers. *The International Journal of the Addictions*, 1976, *11*, 309-24.

Kolb, L. Drug addiction in its relation to crime. *Mental Hygiene*, 1925, *9*, 74-89.

Kolb, L. Types and characteristics of drug addicts. *Mental Hygiene*, 1925, *9*, 300-13.

Kolb, L. *Drug Addiction, a Medical Problem*. Springfield, Ill.: C. C. Thomas, 1962.

Kolb, L., and A. G. du Mez. The prevalence and trend of drug addiction in the United States and factors influencing it. *Public Health Reports*, Reprint 924, 1924.

Kolb, L., and C. K. Himmelsbach. Clinical studies of drug addiction: a critical review of withdrawal treatment with method of evaluating abstinence signs. *Public Health Reports Supp.* No. 128, 1938.

Kuh, R. H. Dealing with narcotics addiction. *New York Law Journal, 144*, June 8-10, 1960.

Kurland, A. A., L. McCabe, and T. Hanlon. Contingent naloxone treatment of the narcotic addict. *The International Journal of the Addictions*, 1976, *11*, 117-130.

Levengood, R. Heroin addiction in the suburbs: an epidemologic study. *American Journal of Public Health*, 1973, 209-14.

Lindesmith, A. R. *Opiate Addiction*. Bloomington, Ind.: Principia Press, 1947.

Lindesmith, A. R. The British system of narcotic control. *Law and Contemporary Problems*, 1957, *22*, 138-54.

Louria, D. B. The major medical problems of heroin addiction. *Annals of Internal Medicine*, 1967, July, pp. 1-22.

MacDonaugh, T. S. The relative effectiveness of a medical hospitalization program vs. a feedback behavior modification program in treating alcohol and drug abusers. *The International Journal of the Addictions*, 1976, *11*, 269-82.

Masserman, J. H. *Principles of Dynamic Psychiatry*. Philadelphia: Saunders, 1946.

Merry, J. Characteristics of addiction to heroin, *British Journal of Addiction*, 1972, *67*, 322-25.

Merrill, F. T. *Japan and the Opium Menace*. New York: Institute of Pacific Relations, 1942.

Meyer, A. S. *Social and Psychological Factors in Opiate Addiction*. New York: Bureau of Applied Social Research, Columbia University, 1952.

Mintz, J., Kate O'Hare, C. P. O'Brien, and Jean Goldschmidt. Sexual problems of heroin addicts. *Archives of General Psychiatry*, 1974, *31*, 700-3.

New York Academy of Medicine, Committee on Public Health, Subcommittee on Drug Addiction. *Bulletin, New York Academy of Medicine*, 1955, *31*, 592-607.

New York City Board of Education. *Suggestions for Teaching the Nature and Effects of Narcotics for Use in Grades 7-12*. New York: Board of Education, 1951.

Nyswander, Marie E. *The Drug Addict as a Patient*. New York: Grune & Stratton, 1956.

New York Times, June 19, 1975.

Payne, E. G. *The Menace of Narcotic Drugs*. New York: Prentice-Hall, 1931.

Pescor, M. J. A statistical analysis of the clinical records of hospitalized drug addicts. *Public Health Reports, Supplement* No. 143, 1938.

Pescor, M. J. The Kolb classification of drug addicts. Supplement No. 155 to the *Public Health Reports*, 1939.

Pescor, M. J. Follow-up study of treated drug addicts. *Public Health Reports Supp.*, No. 170, 1943.

Plag, J. A., et al. Characteristics of naval recruits with histories of drug abuse. *Military Medicine*, 1975, *138*, 354-59.

Platt, J. J., A. R. Hoffman, and E. K. Ebert. Recent trends in the demography of heroin addiction among youthful offenders. *The International Journal of the Addictions*, 1976, *11*, 221-36.

Proceedings of the Third National Conference on Methadone Treatment. New York City, 1970.

Rangini, J., D. Chisolm, M. Glaser, and T. Kappeler. Self-regulated methadone detoxification of heroin addicts: an improved technique in an in-patient setting. *Archives of General Psychiatry*, 1975, *32* 909-11.

Rado, S. The psychoanalysis of pharmacothymia (drug addiction). *Psychoanalytical Quarterly*, 1933, *2*, 1-23.

Research Center for Human Relations, New York University. *Report No. 11, Personal Background of Drug Users, Delinquents and Controls*. New York: New York University, 1957.

Robbins, Lee N., J. E. Helzer, and Darlene H. Davis. Narcotic use in Southeast Asia and afterward. *Archives of General Psychiatry*, 1975, *32*, 955-61.

Romond, Anne M., Catherine K. Forrest, and H. D. Kleber. Follow-up of participants in a drug dependent therapeutic community. *Archives of General Psychiatry*, 1975, *32*, 369-74.

Sabath, G. Some trends in the treatment and epidemiology of drug addiction: Psychotherapy and Synanon. *Psychotherapy: Theory, Research and Practice*, 1967, *4*, 92-96.

Santen, R. J., J. Sofsky, B. Nedjeles, and R. Lippert. Mechanism of action of narcotics in the production of menstrual dysfunction in women. *Fertility and Sterility*, 1975, *26*, 538-47.

Schur, E. M. *Narcotic Addiction in Britain and America*. Bloomington, Ind.: Indiana University Press, 1962.

Select Committee on Crime, U.S. House of Representatives. *First Report on Marijuana*, April 6, 1970. Washington, D.C.: U.S. Government Printing Office, 1970.

Sheffer, A., M. Quinones, M. A. Lavenhar, K. Doyle, and H. Prager. An evaluation of detoxification as an initial step in the treatment of drug addiction. *American Journal of Psychiatry*, 1976, *133*, 337-40.

Smart, G. Outcome studies of therapeutic community and halfway house treatment for addicts. *The International Journal of the Addictions*, 1976, *11*, 143-49.

Smart, R. G., Dianne Fejer, D. Smith, and W. J. White. *Trends in Drug Use among Metropolitan Toronto High School Students: 1968-1974:* Toronto: Addiction Research Foundation of Ontario, 1974.

Spensley, J. Doxepin: A useful adjunct in the treatment of heroin addicts in a methadone program. *The International Journal of the Addictions*, 1976, *11*, 191-97.

Spragg, S. D. S. Morphine addiction in chimpanzees. *Comparative Psychology Monographs*, 1940, *15*, 1-132.

Stone, M. Pregnant addicts—hooked babies. Unpublished paper. New York Medical College, 1974.

Suffet, F., and R. Brotman. Female drug use: some observations. *The International Journal of the Addictions, 1976, 11*, 1-18.

Sutker, P. B., and A. W. Alain. Incarcerated and street heroin addicts: a personality comparison. *Psychological Reports*, 1973, *32*, 243-46.

Tatum, A. L., M. H. Seevers, and K. H. Collins. Morphine addiction and its physiological interpretation based on experimental evidence. *Journal of Pharmacology and Experimental Therapeutics*, 1939, *36*, 447-75.

Tennant, F. S., et al. Heroin detoxification: a comparison of propoxyphene and methadone. *Journal of the American Medical Association*, 1975, *232*, 1019-22.

Terry, C., and M. Pellens. *The opium problem*. New York: Committee on Drug Addiction, Bureau of Social Hygiene, 1926.

References   153

Treadway, W. L. *Further observations on the epidemiology of narcotic drug addiction.* Reprint No. 1359, Public Health Reports. Washington, D.C.: U.S. Government Printing Office, 1930.

Trussell, R. E. *Proceedings, White House Conference on Narcotic and Drug Abuse,* 1962.

Trussell, R. E. *Proceedings, Second National Conference on Narcotic and Drug Abuse,* New York, October, 1969.

United Nations Economic and Social Council, Commission on Narcotic Drugs, *Summary of Annual Reports of Governments,* 1959.

Vaillant, G. E. A twelve-year follow-up study of New York narcotic addicts. *American Journal of Psychiatry,* 1963, *122,* 729-30.

Vogel, V. H., H. Isbell and K. Chapman. Present status of narcotic addiction. *Journal of the American Medical Association,* 1948, *138,* 1019-26.

Wikler, A. Treatment of drug addiction; conferences on therapy. *New York State Journal of Medicine,* 1944, *44,* 1-8.

Wikler, A. Sites and mechanisms of action of morphine and related drugs in the central nervous system. *Journal of Pharmacology and Experimental Therapeutics,* Part II, 1950, *100,* 435-506.

Wikler, A. A psychodynamic study of a patient during experimental self-regulated readdiction to morphine. *Psychiatric Quarterly,* 1952, *26,* 270-93.

Wikler, A. *Opiate Addiction.* Springfield, Ill.: C. C. Thomas, 1953.

Wikler, A. The search for the psyche in drug dependence: a 35 year retrospective study. *Journal of Nervous and Mental Diseases,* 1977, *165,* 29-40.

Wikler, A., and J. Masserman. The effects of morphine on learned adaptive responses and experimental neuroses in cats. *Archives of Neurology and Psychiatry,* 1943, *50,* 401-4.

Winick, C. Narcotics addiction and its treatment. *Law and Contemporary Problems,* 1957, *22,* 9-33.

Winick, C. The 35 to 40 age drop-off. In *Proceedings of the White House Conference on Narcotic and Drug Abuse.* Washington, D.C.: United States Government Printing Office, 1963.

Wolff, H. G., J. D. Hardy, and H. Goodell. Studies on pain. A new method for measuring pain threshold. Observations on spatial summations of pain. *Journal of Clinical Investigation,* 1940, *19,* 649-57.

Zimmerman, P., et al. Heroin addiction in adolescent boys. *Journal of Nervous and Mental Diseases,* 1951, *114,* 19-34.

Zimmering, P., et al. Drug addiction in relation to problems of adolescence. *American Journal of Psychiatry,* 1952, *109,* 272-78.

Nonopiate Addiction

Adamec, C., R. O. Pihl, and L. Leiter. An analysis of the subjective marihuana experience. *The International Journal of the Addictions.* 1976, *11,* 283-94.

Ausubel, D. P. Comment on Dr. Robbins' paper: The long-term effects of marihuana use in adolescents. In *Psychopathology of Adolescence* (J. Zubin and A. Freedman, eds.). New York: Grune & Stratton, 1970, 179-80.

Beaubrun, M. H., and F. Knight. Psychiatric assessment of 30 chronic users of cannabis and 30 matched controls. *American Journal of Psychiatry,* 1973, *130,* 309-11.

Becker, H. S. Becoming a marihuana user. *American Journal of Sociology,* 1953, *59,* 235-42.

Becker, H. S. Marihuana: a sociological overview. In *The Marihuana Papers* (D. Solomon, ed.). New York: Signet Books, 1968, 65-102.

Brecher, E. M., and the Editors of the Consumers Union. *Licit and Illicit Drugs.* Mt. Vernon, N.Y.: Consumers Union, 1972.

Brill, Q., and R. L. Christie. Marihuana use and psychosocial adaptation. *Archives of General Psychiatry,* 1974, *31,* 713-19.

Brill, N. Q., E. Crumpton, and H. M. Grayson. Personality factors in marihuana use. *Archives of General Psychiatry,* 1971, *24,* 163-65.

Charen, S., and L. Perlman. Personality studies of marihuana addicts. *American Journal of Psychiatry,* 1946, *102,* 674-82.

Chopra, R. N., and G. S. Chopra. *The Present Position of Hemp-Drug Addiction in India.* Calcutta, India: Thacker, Spink, 1933.

Chopra, R. N., and G. S. Chopra. Cannabis sativa in relation to mental diseases and crime in India. *Indian Journal of Medical Research,* January 1942.

Cohen, S. Lysergic acid diethylamide: side effects and complications. *Journal of Nervous Diseases,* 1960, *130,* 30-40.

Cohen, S. *The Beyond Within: The LSD Story.* New York: Athaeneum Press, 1968.

Gaskill, H. S. Marihuana, an intoxicant. *American Journal of Psychiatry,* 1945, *102,* 202-04.

Goode, E. (ed.). *Marihuana.* New York: Atherton Press, 1970.

Goode, E. *Drugs in American Society.* New York: Knopf, 1972.

Halikas, J. A., D. W. Goodwin, and S. B. Guze. Marihuana use and psychiatric illness. *Archives of General Psychiatry,* 1972, *27,* 162-65.

Hochman, J. S., and N. O. Brill. Chronic marihuana use and psychosocial adaptation. *American Journal of Psychiatry,* 1973, *140,* 130-32.

Jaffe, J. J. Narcotics and analgesics. Drug addiction and drug abuse. In *The Pharmacological Basis of Therapeutics* (L. Goodman and A. Gilman, eds.). New York: Macmillan, 1970, 237-75; 276-313.

Kandel, Denise. Inter- and intragenerational influences on adolescent marihuana use. *Journal of Social Issues,* 1974, *30,* 107-35.

Kandel, Denise, and R. Faust. Sequence and stages in patterns of adolescent drug use. *Archives of General Psychiatry,* 1975, *32,* 923-32.

Kolansky, H., and W. T. Moore. Toxic effects of chronic marihuana use. *Journal of the American Medical Association,* 1972, *222,* 35-41.

Merrill, F. T. *Marihuana, the New Dangerous Drug.* Washington, D.C.: Opium Research Committee, 1950.

Nahas, G. N. Marihuana. *Journal of the American Medical Association,* 1975, *233,* 79-80.

National Commission on Marihuana and Drug Abuse. *Marihuana: A Signal of Misunderstanding.* Washington, D.C.: U.S. Government Printing Office, 1972.

Kohn, P. M. A functionalist approach to youthful drug use. Paper presented to the American Psychological Association, September 1, 1978, Toronto, Canada.

New York City Mayor's Committee on Marihuana Problem in the City of New York. Lancaster, Pa.: Jacques Cattell Press, 1944.

Payne, R. J., and S. N. Brand. The toxicity of intravenously used marihuana. *Journal of the American Medical Association,* 1975, *233,* 351-54.

Placidyl package insert, rev. June 1971, Abbott Laboratories, North Chicago, Illinois.

Robbins, Lee J., Harriet S. Darvish, and G. E. A. Murphy. Follow-up study of 76 users and 146 nonusers. In *Psychopathology of Adolescence.* (J. Zubin and A. Freeman, eds.). New York: Grune & Stratton, 1970, 159-78.

Rouse, Beatrice, and J. A. Ewing. Marihuana and other drug use by women college students: Associated risk taking and coping activities. *American Journal of Psychiatry,* 1973, *130,* 486-91.

Select Committee on Crime, U.S. House of Representatives. *First Report on Marihuana,* April 6, 1970. Washington, D.C.: U.S. Government Printing Office, 1970.

Single, E., Denise Kandel, and R. Faust. Patterns of multiple drug use in high school. *Journal of Health and Social Behavior,* 1974, *15,* 344-57.

Smart, R. G., et al. *Lysergic acid Diethylamide (LSD) in the Treatment of Alcoholism: An Investigation into its Effects on Drinking Behavior, Personality Structure, and Social Functioning.* Toronto: University of Toronto Press, 1967.

Solomon, D. (ed.). *The Marihuana Papers.* New York: Bobbs-Merrill, 1966.

Valium package insert, September 1971, Roche Laboratories, Nutley, N. J.

Walton, R. P. *Marihuana: America's New Drug Problem.* Philadelphia: Lippincott, 1938.

Index

157